1st EDITION

Perspectives on Diseases and Disorders

Autism

Carrie Fredericks
Book Editor

GREENHAVEN PRESS
A part of Gale, Cengage Learning

Detroit • New York • San Francisco • New Haven, Conn • Waterville, Maine • London

© 2008 Gale, a part of Cengage Learning

For more information, contact:
Greenhaven Books
27500 Drake Rd.
Farmington Hills, MI 48331-3535
Or you can visit our Internet site at gale.cengage.com

Cover photo: © Michael Macor/San Francisco Chronicle/Corbis

LIBRARY OF CONGRESS CATALOGING-IN-PUBLICATION DATA

Autism / Carrie Fredericks, book editor.
    p. cm. — (Perspectives on diseases and disorders)
Includes bibliographical references and index.
ISBN-13: 978-0-7377-3869-8 (hardcover)
1. Autism—Popular works. I. Fredericks, Carrie.
RC553.A88A826 2008
616.85'882—dc22   2007037472

ISBN-10: 0-7377-3869-3

Printed in the United States of America
3 4 5 6 7 12 11 10 09 08

CONTENTS

INTRODUCTION

Autism, a lifelong disorder, is defined as a behavioral and neurological disorder affecting physical, language, and social skills. Currently there is no known cause or cure for any of the autism spectrum disorders—a group of disorders categorized as developmental disabilities—though many studies have focused on genetic links to autism.

Autism is largely characterized by impairment in social communication and interaction; those with autism often display repetitive behaviors and mannerisms. Four times more boys than girls have the disorder, but girls are often affected more severely. Autism can come in many forms, from high-functioning autistics, as in those with Asperger's Syndrome, to low-functioning individuals who have minimal communication or social skills. Higher-functioning autistics can exhibit several characteristics that indicate a higher form of the disorder: acquiring language before age six, IQ levels above 50, and showing an affinity to a particular skill (like computers or music). Lower-functioning autistics may have no social or communication skills and may also have some form of mental retardation.

Autism spectrum disorders are likely caused by a genetic vulnerability that is triggered by an unknown factor or factors. Many researchers have theorized that such factors include external or environmental triggers. Genetic mutations can take many years to manifest themselves, making the likelihood of environmental triggers even stronger. Prior to 1980 no diagnostic standards for autism existed, and any diagnosis was based on the individual physician. With the fourth edition of the *Diagnostic and*

Statistical Manual of Mental Disorders (DSM-IV) standards in place as of 2000, autism diagnosis is based on specific criteria and characteristics, leading to concentrated research into the factors triggering autism spectrum disorders.

Research into the causes of autism has advanced greatly in the last several years and revealed new evidence of biomedical causes. In July 2006 a study done at the

Students challenged by autism, mental retardation, and other disabilities are taught how to keep balance in order to learn to dance. (**AP Images.**)

University of California at Davis showed males with autism have fewer neurons (nerve cells) in the section of the brain that processes memory and emotion. More study on this area of the brain (the amygdala) will be needed to clarify whether autistic males are born with fewer neurons or whether something occurs early in life to cause neuron loss. In 2006 a study of one hundred children with autism spectrum disorders found a small group had unusually low cholesterol levels. This finding has led researchers to theorize that cholesterol may be causally connected to autism in some cases.

Genetic Research Gaining Ground

Genetic research into autism causes has focused on several different areas. A study done at the University of California at Los Angeles has pointed to an autism gene on chromosome 17. This genetic possibility was found only in families with males that have autism, which could explain the predisposition of males to have the disorder. Another explanation for this predisposition may by found in a genetic study at the University of Washington which has shown that autism may be caused by different genes for boys than for girls. Another genetic study through Vanderbilt University focused on 743 families who had at least one child with autism. The study found a difference in the genetic makeup of some families that was associated with a doubled risk of having autism. In a 2006 article by Doug Brunk in *Pediatric News*, the International Medical News Group, reports, "They found that people with two copies of the MET gene variant were 2.27 times more likely to have autism as were people in the general population. The risk of autism among study participants who had only one copy of the variant was also high: a relative risk of 1.67 compared with the general population." A new study at the Cold Spring Harbor Laboratory in New York has shown that genetic causes of autism may be far more complicated than originally thought. The study compared the genes of autistic children to the genes of their parents to see if any mutations had occurred between generations and found very small changes in a large number of genes. These findings could change the direction of future autism research.

Autism Studies Reveal Possible Causes

At the University of California at Davis, researchers are overseeing a study called CHARGE, Childhood Autism Risks from Genetics and the Environment. The researchers hope to find genetic or environmental patterns that would help explain how autism happens. Joshua Tompkins, a journalist with *Popular Science*, writes in a 2005 article, "Churning through reams of data, the study has uncovered its first pattern: that certain proteins, metabolites and immune system components in blood samples from autistic children differ sharply from normal ones." A study done through Johns Hopkins University on seven hundred Danish children has shown outside factors possibly becoming more evident. Tompkins writes, "Some intriguing correlations emerged. Scouring for trends among a host of parameters such as birth weight and socioeconomic status, scientists discovered an increased prevalence of autism both in children with a family history of schizophrenia and in those whose births involved complications such as premature or breech delivery."

One of the largest studies in the history of autism, the Autism Genome Project, includes more than 120 scientists from nineteen countries. This study has produced a genome scan to help collect autism DNA for further research; the genome, encoded in the DNA, is all the hereditary information an organism possesses. The Autism Genome Project looked for common genetic factors in almost twelve hundred families and showed that autism risk seems to be clustered in the area of chromosome 11. The study also found a possible aberration in a biological process involving glutamate, an important molecule in cellular metabolism. In February 2007 Neil Osterweil, senior associate editor of *MedPage Today* reported, "There is also evidence that chromosomal abnormalities or genetic disorders such as fragile X syndrome or tuberous sclerosis syndrome, both of which involve aberrant glutamate signaling, may be involved in autism risk."

Another outside factor being considered as an autism cause is television viewing, an activity done by most people, even very small children. A study by Cornell University economists using cable subscription data and rainfall data (more TV is watched when it is raining) showed autism rising at rates that correspond to rising cable subscriptions. Since no actual television viewing was studied, however, some have questioned whether this information points to a cause. Vanderbilt University geneticist Paul Levitt states in a 2006 *Time* article by Claudia Wallis, "How do you know, for instance, that it's not mold or mildew in the counties that have a lot of rain?"

A Cure for Autism?

Many have wondered where all this research leads, asking whether a complete and total cure for autism spectrum disorders can or should be found. Many important figures in history displayed characteristics of autism: Albert Einstein; Alan Turing, known as the father of modern computing; gorilla researcher Dian Fossey; Lewis Carroll, the author of *Alice's Adventures in Wonderland*; Sir Isaac Newton; Barbara McClintock, a Nobel Prize–winning geneticist who discovered how to tell the difference between groups of genes called chromosomes; author Hans Christian Andersen; comedian Andy Kaufman; and Thomas Jefferson, to name a few. Some people believe that completely curing autism would deprive the world of many great individuals and skills. In the summer of 2006 researchers in England applied to the British government to begin using preimplantation diagnosis

(PGD) to screen embryos for autism. If any markers of autism risk factors were found, this would allow doctors to implant only female embryos during in vitro fertilization, since the majority of autistics are male. In a 2006 article at LifeSiteNews.com, Hilary White quotes bioethicist Ben Mitchell as saying, "If unborn children are being eliminated for a genetic disposition to autism, no one is safe. . . . Today autism, tomorrow intelligence below 70 I.Q., the next day male pattern baldness."

Jim Sinclair, a man with autism, states that autism is not something a person has; autism is a way of being, and if you take the autism out of the person, the person left is not the same one as before. Many autistic individuals would not get rid of their autism if given the opportunity. Temple Grandin, one of the most well-known autistics today, states at her Web site, "If I could snap my fingers and be nonautistic, I would not—because then I wouldn't be me. Autism is a part of who I am." Author Stephen M. Shore writes in his 2006 book *Understanding Autism for Dummies*, "Fortunately, I am able to successfully use my set of characteristics, which we refer to as autism, and do not wish to be 'cured' out of a fulfilling and productive life. However, we are duty bound to help persons more severely affected with autism to lead fruitful lives to their greatest potential by using their strengths." As researchers continue the study of autism, perhaps someday soon the more severe symptoms and neurological damage of autism can be controlled, leaving autistic individuals the freedom to pursue their own lives, in their own way, with their own particular set of skills.

CHAPTER 1

Understanding Autism

An Overview of Autism

Carol A. Turkington

In the following selection Carol A. Turkington provides an overview of autism that covers causes of the disorder, diagnosis, treatments, and prognosis. Autism spectrum disorders include several different disorders that involve problems with the senses, communication, and socialization. As the rate of autism continues to rise, the disorder is becoming more well known and better studied. While no cure for this lifelong disorder exists, therapies ease symptoms across the whole spectrum of disabilities, from the severe to the highly functioning individual. Turkington is a medical writer and editor.

Photo on previous page. Jeanne Marshall, chief training officer at the Judevine Center for Autism, talks about some of the services offered by the center. (**AP Images.**)

Autism is a severe disorder of brain function marked by problems with social contact, intelligence and language, together with ritualistic or compulsive behavior and bizarre responses to the environment.

SOURCE: Carol A Turkington, *The Gale Encyclopedia of Medicine,* Third Edition, Farmington Hills, MI: Thomson Gale, 2006. Reproduced by permission of Gale a part of Cengage Learning.

Description of Autism

Autism is a lifelong disorder that interferes with the ability to understand what is seen, heard, and touched. This can cause profound problems in personal behavior and in the ability to relate to others. A person with autism must learn how to communicate normally and how to relate to people, objects and events. However, not all patients suffer the same degree of impairment. There is a full spectrum of symptoms, which can range from mild to severe.

Autism occurs in as many as one or two per 1,000 children. It is found four times more often in boys (usually the first-born) and occurs around the world in all races and social backgrounds. Autism usually is evident in the first three years of life, although in some children it's hard to tell when the problem develops. Sometimes the condition isn't diagnosed until the child enters school.

While a person with autism can have symptoms ranging from mild to severe, about 10% have an extraordinary ability in one area, such as in mathematics, memory, music, or art. Such children are known as "autistic savants" (formerly known as "idiot savants").

Causes of Autism

Autism is a brain disorder that affects the way the brain uses or transmits information. Studies have found abnormalities in several parts of the brain that almost certainly occurred during fetal development. The problem may be centered in the parts of the brain responsible for processing language and information from the senses.

There appears to be a strong genetic basis for autism. Identical twins are more likely to both be affected than twins who are fraternal (not genetically identical). In a family with one autistic child, the chance of having another child with autism is about 1 in 20, much higher than in the normal population. Sometimes, relatives of an autistic child have mild behaviors that look very much like autism, such as repetitive behaviors and social or communication problems. Research also has found that some emotional disorders (such as manic depression) occur more often in families of a child with autism.

At least one group of researchers has found a link between an abnormal gene and autism. The gene may be just one of at least three to five genes that interact in some way to cause the condition. Scientists suspect that a faulty gene or genes might make a person vulnerable to develop autism in the presence of other factors, such as a chemical imbalance, viruses or chemicals, or a lack of oxygen at birth.

In a few cases, autistic behavior is caused by a disease such as:

- rubella in the pregnant mother
- tuberous sclerosis
- fragile X syndrome
- encephalitis
- untreated phenylketonuria

The severity of the condition varies between individuals, ranging from the most severe (extremely unusual, repetitive, self-injurious, and aggressive behavior) to very mild, resembling a personality disorder with some learning disability.

Symptoms of Autism

Profound problems with social interaction are the most common symptoms of autism. Infants with the disorder won't cuddle; they avoid eye contact and don't seem to want or need physical contact or affection. They may become rigid or flaccid when they are held, cry when picked up, and show little interest in human contact. Such a child doesn't smile or lift his arms in anticipation of being picked up. He forms no attachment to parents nor shows any normal anxiety toward strangers. He doesn't learn typical games of childhood, such as peek-a-boo.

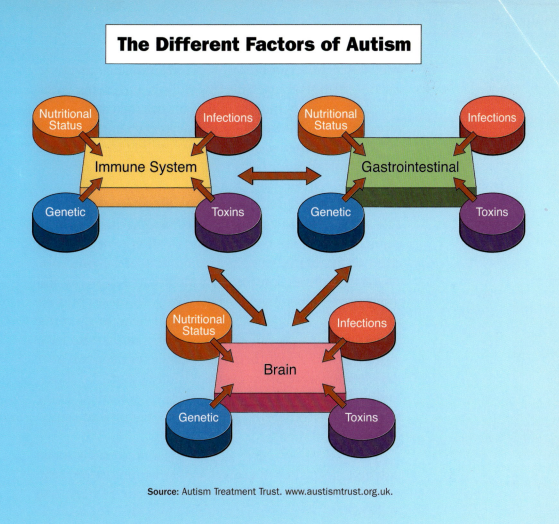

The Different Factors of Autism

Immune System
Nutritional Status
Infections
Genetic
Toxins

Gastrointestinal
Nutritional Status
Infections
Genetic
Toxins

Brain
Nutritional Status
Infections
Genetic
Toxins

Source: Autism Treatment Trust. www.austismtrust.org.uk.

The child with autism may not speak at all; if he does, it is often in single words. He may endlessly repeat words or phrases that are addressed to him and may reverse pronouns ("You go sleep" instead of "I want to go to sleep").

Activity and Play

Usually a child with autism has many problems playing normally. He probably won't act out adult roles during play time, and instead of enjoying fantasy play, he may simply repeatedly mimic the actions of someone else. Bizarre behavior patterns are very common among autistic children and may include complex rituals, screaming fits, rhythmic rocking, arm flapping, finger twiddling, and crying without tears. Autistic children may play with their own saliva, feces or urine. They may be self-destructive, biting their own hands, gouging at their eyes, pulling their hair, or banging their head.

Sensory and Intellectual Problems

The sensory world poses a real problem to many autistic children, who seem overwhelmed by their own senses. A child with autism may ignore objects or become obsessed with them, continually watching the object or the movement of his fingers over it. Many of these children may react to sounds by banging their head or flapping fingers. Some high-functioning autistic adults who have written books about their childhood experiences report that sounds were often excruciatingly painful to them, forcing them to withdraw from their environment or try to cope by withdrawing into their own world of sensation and movement.

Most autistic children appear to be moderately mentally retarded. They may giggle or cry for no reason, have no fear of real danger, but exhibit terror of harmless objects.

Diagnosis of Autism

There is no medical test for autism. Because the symptoms of autism are so varied, the condition may go undiagnosed for some time (especially in those with mild cases or if other handicaps are also present). It may be confused with other diseases, such as fragile X syndrome, tuberous sclerosis, and untreated phenylketonuria.

Autism is diagnosed by observing the child's behavior, communication skills, and social interactions. Medical tests should rule out other possible causes of autistic symptoms. Criteria that mental health experts use to diagnose autism include:

- problems with developing friendships
- problems with make-believe or social play
- endlessly repeated words or strings of words
- difficulty in carrying on a conversation
- obsessions with rituals or restricted patterns
- preoccupation with parts of objects

Some children have a few of the symptoms of autism, but not enough to be diagnosed with the "classical" form

A trained specialist can diagnosis autism by observing a child's behavior, social interactions and communication skills. **(Bernard Bisson/ Sygma/Corbis)**

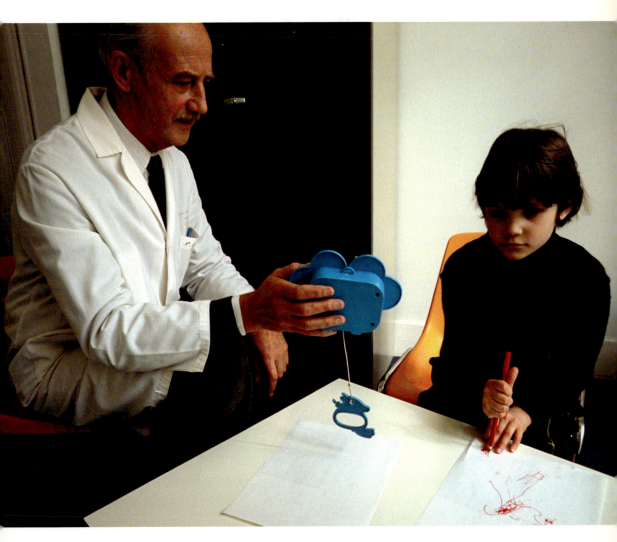

of the condition. Children who have autistic behavior but no problems with language may be diagnosed with "Asperger syndrome." Children who seem normal at first but who begin to show autistic behavior as they get older might be diagnosed with "childhood disintegrative disorder" (CDD). These problems are sometimes called "autistic spectrum disorders." It is also important to rule out other problems that seem similar to autism.

Methods of Treatment

There is no cure for autism. Treatments are aimed at reducing specific symptoms. Because the symptoms vary so widely from one person to the next, there is not a single approach that works for every person. A spectrum of interventions include training in music, listening, vision, speech and language, and senses. Special diets and medications may also be prescribed.

Studies show that people with autism can improve significantly with proper treatment. A child with autism can learn best with special teachers in a structured program that emphasizes individual instruction. The two most-often studied types of treatment are [educational or behavioral treatment and medication].

Typically, behavioral techniques are used to help the child respond and decrease symptoms. This might include positive reinforcement (food and rewards) to boost language and social skills. This training includes structured, skill-oriented instruction designed to boost social and language abilities. Training needs to begin as early as possible, since early intervention appears to influence brain development.

Most experts believe that modern treatment is most effective when carried out at home, although treatment may also take place in a psychiatric hospital, specialized school, or day care program.

> **FAST FACT**
>
> In about 5 percent of autism cases another disorder is also present.

No single medication has yet proved highly effective for the major features of autism. However, a variety of drugs can control self-injurious, aggressive, and other of the more difficult behaviors. Drugs also can control epilepsy, which afflicts up to 20% of people with autism.

Five types of drugs are sometimes prescribed to help the behavior problems of people with autism:

- stimulants, such as methylphenidate (Ritalin)
- antidepressants, such as fluroxamine (Luvox)
- opiate blockers, such as naltrexone (ReVia)
- antipsychotics
- tranquilizers.

Today, most experts recommend a complex treatment regimen that begins early and continues through the teenage years. Behavioral therapies are used in conjunction with medications.

Alternative Treatment

Many parents report success with megavitamin therapy. Some studies have shown that vitamin B6 improves eye contact and speech and lessens tantrum behavior. Vitamin B6 causes fewer side effects than other medications and is considered safe when used in appropriate doses. However, not many health practitioners advocate its use in the treatment of autism, citing that the studies showing its benefit were flawed.

[The] compound [DMG (dimethylglycine)], available in many health food stores, is legally classified as a food, not a vitamin or drug. Some researchers claim that it improves speech in children with autism. Those who respond to this treatment will usually do so within a week. Again, many doctors do not feel that the studies are adequate to promote this treatment.

One researcher found that vigorous exercise (20 minutes or longer, three or four days a week) seems to decrease hyperactivity, aggression, self-injury and other autistic symptoms.

Prognosis

While there is no cure, with appropriate treatment the negative behaviors of autism may improve. Earlier generations placed autistic children in institutions; today, even severely disabled children can be helped in a less restrictive environment to develop to their highest potential. Many can eventually become more responsive to others as they learn to understand the world around them, and some can lead nearly normal lives.

People with autism have a normal life expectancy. Some people with autism can handle a job; they do best with structured jobs that involve a degree of repetition.

Until the cause of autism is discovered, prevention is not possible.

Signs and Diagnosis of Autism

Kathleen A. Fergus

According to Kathleen A. Fergus individuals with autism can have a wide range of differing abilities and needs. When autism is suspected, certain types of telling behaviors can be diagnosed, including problems in communication skills, social interaction, and play. In addition, repetitive motions, temper tantrums, overstimulation, and hyperactivity can also be present. A lack of physical findings in individuals with autism makes diagnosis more difficult. According to the *Diagnostic and Statistical Manual of Mental Disorders* (*DSM IV*), specific criteria can be used to pinpoint the diagnosis of autism. Observation and evaluation by a medical specialist is critical to getting an accurate diagnosis. Fergus has degrees in cell and molecular biology and genetic counseling. She is the author of many health and genetics-related articles.

One of the most frustrating aspects of autism is the lack of physical findings in individuals with autism. Most individuals with autism have nor-

SOURCE: Kathleen A Fergus, *The Gale Encyclopedia of Genetic Disorders*, Farmington Hills, MI: Thomson Gale, 2005. Reproduced by permission of Gale a part of Cengage Learning.

mal appearances, and few, if any, medical problems. Because the specific cause of autism is unknown, there is no prenatal test available for autism.

Autism is a spectrum disorder. A spectrum refers to the fact that different individuals with a diagnosis of autism can have very different abilities and deficits. The spectrum of autism stretches from a socially isolated adult with normal IQ to a severely affected child with mental retardation and behavioral problems. The following is a partial list of behaviors seen in individuals with autism divided into main areas of concern. It is unlikely that any one individual would exhibit all of the following behaviors. Most affected people would be expected to exhibit some but not all of the behaviors.

Autistic Behaviors

In the area of communication skills, behaviors autistic individuals may display include:

- language delay or absence
- impaired speech
- meaningless repetition of words or phrases
- using gestures rather than words to communicate
- concrete or literal understanding of words or phrases
- inability to initiate or hold conversations

In the area of social interaction, behaviors autistic individuals may display include:

- unresponsiveness to people
- lack of attachment to parents or caregivers
- little or no interest in human contact
- failure to establish eye contact
- little interest in making friends
- unresponsiveness to social cues such as smiles or frowns

In the area of play, behaviors autistic individuals may display include:

- little imaginative play
- play characterized by repetition (e.g., endless spinning of car wheels)
- no desire for group play
- no pretend games

Autistic individuals may display behaviors that include:

- repetitive motions such as hand flapping and head banging
- rigid or flaccid muscle tone when held
- temper tantrums or screaming fits
- resistance to change
- hyperactivity
- fixates or develops obsessive interest in an activity, idea, or person
- overreaction to sensory stimulus such as noise, lights, and texture
- inappropriate laughing or giggling

Diagnosing Autism

There is no medical test, such as a blood test or brain scan to diagnose autism. The diagnosis of autism is very difficult to make in young children due to the lack of physical findings and the variable behavior of children. Because the primary signs and symptoms of autism are behavioral, the diagnosis usually requires evaluation by a specialized team of health professionals and occurs over a period of time. This team of specialists may include a developmental pediatrician, speech therapist, psychologist, geneticist, and other health professionals. Medical tests may be done to rule out other possible causes and may include a hearing evaluation, chromosome analysis,

DNA testing for specific genetic disorders, and brain imaging scans, including magnetic resonance imaging (MRI), electroencephalogram (EEG), or computed tomography (CT), to rule out structural brain anomalies.

Once other medical causes have been excluded, the diagnosis for autism can be made using criteria from the

A woman watches her son work with a therapist, relearning how to speak. Diagnosing autism is a complicated process due to the lack of physical findings available. (AP Images.)

fourth edition of the *Diagnostic and Statistical Manual of Mental Disorders* (DSM IV). This manual, developed by the American Psychiatric Association, lists abnormal behaviors in three key areas: impairment in social interaction, impairment in communication (language), and restrictive and repetitive patterns of behavior. These behaviors are usually seen in individuals with autism. If an individual displays enough distinct behaviors from the list, they meet the diagnostic criteria for autism. Most individuals will not exhibit all of the possible behaviors and, while individuals might exhibit the same behaviors, there is still a large degree of variability within this syndrome.

Criteria for Diagnosis

The DSM-IV criteria for a diagnosis of autistic disorder require a display total of at least six behaviors from items 1, 2, and 3, with at least two from 1, and one each from 2 and 3.

Under item 1 in the DSM-IV, the criteria are qualitative impairment in social interaction, as manifested by at least two of the following:

- marked impairment in the use of multiple nonverbal behaviors such as eye-to-eye gaze, facial expression, body postures, and gestures to regulate social interaction

- failure to develop peer relationships appropriate to developmental level

- markedly impaired expression of pleasure in other people's happiness

Under the DSM-IV's item 2, the criteria are qualitative impairments in communication, as manifested by at least one of the following:

- delay in, or total lack of, the development of spoken language (not accompanied by an attempt to

> **FAST FACT**
>
> Characteristic behaviors of autism can become apparent in the first few months after birth, or they may appear at any time during a child's early years.

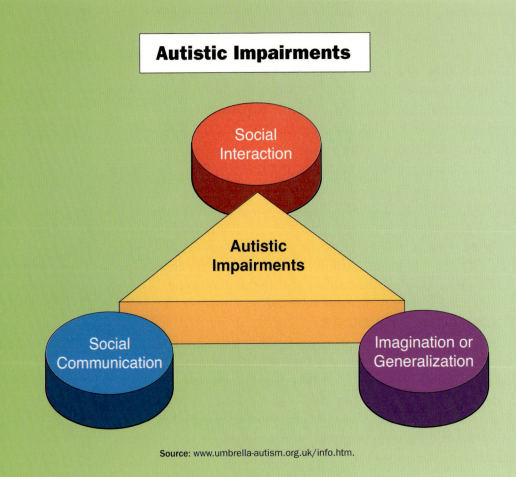

Autistic Impairments

Social Interaction

Autistic Impairments

Social Communication

Imagination or Generalization

Source: www.umbrella-autism.org.uk/info.htm.

compensate through alternative modes of communication such as gestures or mime)

• in individuals with adequate speech, marked impairment in the ability to initiate or sustain a conversation with others

• stereotyped and repetitive use of language or idiosyncratic language

• lack of varied spontaneous make-believe play or social imitative play appropriate to developmental level

Under item 3, the DSM-IV criteria are restricted repetitive and stereotyped patterns of behavior, interests, and activities, as manifested by as least one of the following:

- encompassing preoccupation with one or more stereotyped and restricted patterns of interest that is abnormal either in intensity or focus
- apparently compulsive adherence to specific non-functional routines or rituals
- stereotyped and repetitive motor mannerisms (e.g., hand or finger flapping or twisting, or complex whole-body movements)
- persistent preoccupation with parts of objects

Other criteria that help diagnose autism include delays or abnormal functioning in at least one of the following areas, with onset prior to age three years:

- social interaction
- language as used in social communication
- symbolic or imaginative play

Autism is the usual diagnosis when there is no findings of Rett disorder or childhood disintegrative disorder (CDD).

Timing of an Autistic Diagnosis

Using all these criteria, the diagnosis of autism is usually made in children by approximately the age of two and a half to three; they are originally seen for speech delay. Often these children are initially thought to have hearing impairments due to their lack of response to verbal cues and their lack of speech.

While speech delay or absence of speech might initially bring a child to the attention of medical or educational professionals, it soon becomes apparent that there are other symptoms in addition to the lack of speech. Children with autism are often noticed for their lack of spontaneous play and their lack of initiative in communication. These deficits become more obvious when these children are enrolled in school for the first time. Their inability to interact with their peers becomes highlighted.

Behaviors such as hand flapping, temper tantrums, and head banging also contribute to the diagnosis.

Because the criteria to diagnose autism are based on observation, several appointments with health care providers may be necessary before a definitive diagnosis is reached. A specialist closely observes and evaluates the child's language and social behavior. In addition to observation, structured interviews of the parents are used to elicit information about early behavior and development.

The Causes of Autism

Stephen M. Shore and Linda G. Rastelli

In this selection Stephen M. Shore and Linda G. Rastelli explain the causes of autism. Different types of autism have different symptoms, and researchers do not believe that autism has a single cause, they argue. A strong genetic component exists in a large number of individuals with an autism spectrum disorder. Brain scans have shown differences in the shape and structure of the brain. Another focus on the causes of autism is the gastrointestinal tract. Often called the "second brain," the GI tract has been shown to cause several types of problems in autistic children. The authors also explore several biomedical and environmental theories about what causes autism, including allergies, heavy metals, and viruses. Every day more findings are published as to possible factors in the cause of autism.

Shore has autism and teaches college courses in special education. He also works with autistic children and consults on autism-related issues. He holds several bachelor's degrees and a master's degree. Rastelli is a journalist and author focusing on technical, health, and business topics.

SOURCE: Stephen M. Shore and Linda G. Rastelli, *Understanding Autism for Dummies*. Indianapolis, IN: Wiley Publishing, Inc., 2006. Copyright © 2006 by Wiley Publishing, Inc., Indianapolis, Indiana. Reprinted with permission of John Wiley & Sons, Inc.

Many things about autism remain unknown—including what every parent wants to know upon hearing a diagnosis: the causes of the disorder. We say "causes" rather than "cause" because it's possible—although not definite—that autism has several triggers. Research is still in the early stages, and the complexity of the condition means that scientists can draw very few definite conclusions. As of this writing, researchers have data that suggests correlations—or factors that are related to having autism—rather than data that suggests causation—or factors that would cause autism. The good news is that the U.S. government has increased funding substantially in recent times. The National Institute of Health now [as of 2006] spends close to a billion dollars annually on autism research, up from $22 million as recently as 1997.

Because researchers have identified different types of autism, with different symptoms, they don't believe one theory on the causes will fit all types. Some autistic disorders may be environmental, and some may be entirely genetic. We just don't know. In the absence of any categorical answer for the question of autism's causes, researchers are proposing and debunking theories while they continue to study genetic and environmental factors that may help fill in pieces of the puzzle. . . .

Exploring the Genetic Link

Researchers believe that a genetic component or predisposition is present in the majority of people who develop autism spectrum disorders. They point to irregular segments of genetic code as the culprits for some autism cases.

A genetic predisposition, however, doesn't dictate what may develop. A predisposition isn't the same as a cause. A person can have a genetic predisposition to heart disease or cancer but avoid it by living a careful lifestyle. Genetics doesn't equal destiny. Unfortunately, a person can have a genetic predisposition, lead a healthy lifestyle, and still develop a disorder. The following sections explore the connections between genetics and autism.

Familial Patterns

Research has found that autism clusters in families. The federal Centers for Disease Control and Prevention [CDC] has data showing the following diagnosis rates among family members:

- Identical twins, who have the same genetic makeup, have about a 75-percent concordance rate (meaning that both twins have autism).

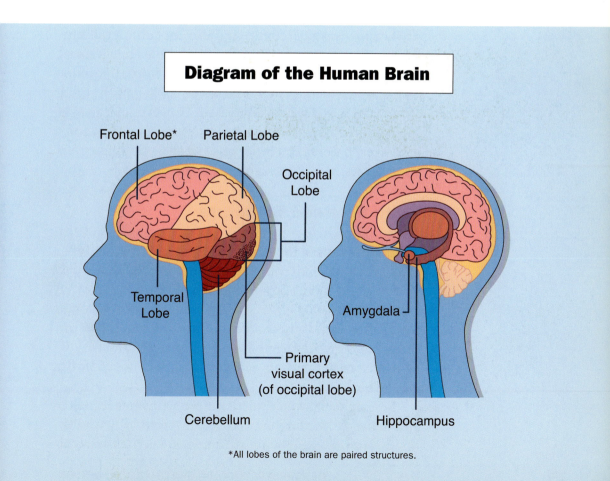

Diagram of the Human Brain

Frontal Lobe*

Parietal Lobe

Occipital Lobe

Temporal Lobe

Amygdala

Primary visual cortex (of occipital lobe)

Cerebellum

Hippocampus

*All lobes of the brain are paired structures.

Source: Stephen M. Shore and Linda G. Rastelli, *Understanding Autism for Dummies*, 2006.

- Fraternal (nonidentical) twins have a 3-percent concordance rate.
- The risk of autism in normal siblings ranges from 2 to 8 percent.
- Among families that contain diagnoses of autism, research shows a 10- to 40-percent increase in the diagnoses of other developmental disabilities, such as language delays and learning disabilities.

Researchers have concluded that families that carry autism genes also carry other conditions in members who don't necessarily have autism. The inheritance pattern for autism spectrum disorders is complex and suggests that mutations in a number of different genes (at least 10) may be involved, according to some research. That explains what Temple Grandin, an author and professor who has autism, calls the "highly variable nature" of autism. Craig Newschaffer at the Johns Hopkins School of Medicine estimates that 60 to 90 percent of all autism cases are genetically based. However, because of the complex nature of autism genetics, scientists don't have a test parents can order to see if their children are at an increased risk of developing the disorder. . . .

Brain Size and Structure

Little is known about the etiology, or origins, of autism. Science has no test for it. But brain scans and other types of research have identified differences in the shape and structure of the brains—particularly in the frontal lobes—of autistic people, including those with Asperger Syndrome. Researchers are scanning DNA to try to put the genetic puzzle together and develop treatments, diagnostic screening tools, and tests that will help identify autism earlier.

Researchers haven't ruled out problems in pregnancy and delivery. Maybe the child gets exposed to neurotoxins (brain cell-destroying substances) such as mercury from contaminated fish, for instance, or experiences damage during the delivery process. These so-called environmental insults, or traumas, can interact with genetics to result in autism. . . .

An abnormality in brain size and structure (along with functioning) is the general consensus for what causes autism, yet researchers don't know exactly which kinds of abnormalities they can attribute to genetics. Researchers at the Autism Tissue Program in Princeton, N.J., which studies donated brain tissue to understand autistic behaviors, say the cause of spectrum disorders could be innate genetic anomalies or environmental insults, or trauma. Research has found abnormalities in the brains of autistic individuals, namely in several neurotransmitter systems (neurotransmitters are the chemical messengers of the brain).

> **FAST FACT**
>
> Autism probably results from abnormalities in at least three to twenty genes and very likely has no single causal gene.

Researchers have found a larger overall brain size (or volume) in autistic children 12 and younger, although the parietal lobes—associated with movement, orientation, recognition, and perception of stimuli—are smaller than normal. The brain is actually often heavier in young children with autism. Also, the amygdala and the hippocampus, the memory center, are larger in autistic children but are the same size or smaller in adolescents and adults. It seems, however, that the connections are missing or not working correctly when the brain tries to process information between different local systems. Imagine that you can call your aunt in the next county, but when you try to call long distance, you can't get a line. This gives you a small taste of what autistic people must deal with.

An overgrowth of nerve connections in the brain, according to one theory, may cause the brain to become overwhelmed with neurotransmitter signals. This theory is consistent with research studies that have found that autistic babies' heads may grow faster than normal at various points. Why would this overgrowth occur? The normal cell "pruning" process of the fetus doesn't occur, and too many neurons exist.

How Does Autism Develop?

Why would genetic abnormalities of the brain lead to autism? This isn't well understood, and researchers have different theories. Some researchers think of autism as a disorder of brain-circuit dysfunction. Researcher Eric Courchesne from the University of California found abnormal growth in the frontal cortexes of autistic brains; he deduced that the only normally functioning parts of the autistic brain are the visual cortex and the areas in the back of the brain that store memories. The frontal cortex is involved with sensory interpretation, which may explain why the visual cortex (responsible for visual perception) functions normally, yet autistic people seem to have visual processing (understanding what they see) issues.

Dr. Margaret Bauman, a pediatric neurologist and director of the LADDERS Clinic at Massachusetts General Hospital believes that the structural problems of the autistic brain are primarily in the limbic system, which includes the amygdala (the emotion center) and the cerebellum, which is associated with the regulation and coordination of movement, posture, and balance. The cerebellum's involvement with a person's motor function could also explain the poor motor skills that individuals on the autism spectrum often display.

John Ratey, MD, author of *The User's Guide to the Brain* and professor of psychiatry at Harvard Medical School, writes that many autistic persons have eye-movement and hearing difficulties and facial-nerve palsy consistent with brainstem injury during their mothers' first trimester of pregnancy.

Other studies show increased cerebellum size, but increased by the same proportion as the brain as a whole.

One study, conducted by [E.H.] Aylward, [N.J.] Minshew, and others found that the cerebrum (and other specific structures) was abnormally large in relation to the size of the brain as a whole.

Some parts of the brain work really well in certain autistic individuals, however. Temple Grandin, an author and professor who has autism, is one example. She has something akin to a videocamera in her head, allowing her to replay images and examine their details. Yet, she feels that other parts of her brain are underdeveloped. For example, she was never able to learn algebra because she couldn't visualize the concepts.

The Brain-Gut Connection

Some researchers have focused on what they call the "second brain": the gut. The nervous system of the upper gastrointestinal, or GI, tract is extremely complex, and not much is known about how it interacts with the brain. This brain/gut connection is the focus of neurogastroenterology.

Dr. Jill James, a professor of pediatrics at the University of Arkansas, and Dr. Richard Deth, a Northeastern University neuropharmacologist, have conducted a preliminary study that found autistic children have great difficulty with what scientists call the methylation process.

Methylation is a metabolic process of making a molecule longer by adding a carbon. It's necessary for regulating DNA synthesis and enzymes, building neurotransmitters, synchronizing neurons, and to make cellular energy.

James's and Deth's work has been interpreted as follows: The faulty methylation process means that autistic people can't eliminate heavy metals such as aluminum, cadmium, lead, and mercury from their systems. Some researchers believe these metals lead to the symptoms of autism.

Problems with methylation may be genetic or environmentally induced, or they may occur through an interaction between genetics and the environment. Such findings are preliminary and require further research.

The Testosterone Link

A theory proposed by a British researcher, Simon Baron-Cohen, explains autism as the result of right-brain dominance, a pattern typically seen in males. He theorizes that too much testosterone in utero leads to the symptoms of autism. Autism, in this theory, is simply being "too male."

Baron-Cohen's research shows that fetuses producing high levels of testosterone may have a higher chance of developing autism. And it seems to be consistent with the fact that autistic boys outnumber autistic girls.

Baron-Cohen believes that the human brain specializes either in empathy (being able to appreciate and understand the emotions of others) or in understanding systems (being able to manipulate data). The former is an E-type brain, and the latter is an S-type brain, and he says that most boys have the S-type brain.

When studying the relationship between empathy and autism, Baron-Cohen found that children who experienced high-prenatal testosterone levels make less eye contact as toddlers and have lower communication skills at age 4, although he concedes that the necessary evidence to prove his theory isn't available. Other researchers have also criticized his work as playing upon stereotypes of girls as good with people and boys as good with objects. Those stereotypes may have some biological basis, but many exceptions to this generalization exist. Another problem with this research is that Baron-Cohen's paradigm doesn't explain all the symptoms of autism.

Examining Biomedical Theories

Researchers suggest that several distinct autistic subtypes exist that differ not necessarily in their symptoms and

A mother and her autistic son sit on the stairs of their home. The boy developed autism symptoms gradually after receiving two childhood vaccinations on the same day after he was fifteen months old. (**AP Images.**)

presentation, but in their causes. Some scientists believe that environmental factors (sometimes coupled with genetic factors) may explain what causes autism and the increase in autism diagnoses. They say that genetic factors alone can't be sufficient for the number of cases seen today; thus, a search for environmental triggers that cause autism in genetically susceptible individuals is underway. . . .

[There are many] theories involving allergies or food intolerances, heavy-metal poisoning, and autoimmune responses and triggers. Researchers are currently investigating all the theories, which means that none of them have enough supporting evidence to say they've been proven correct as of this writing [in 2006]. The problem is establishing that causation [one thing causing something else] is taking place, not simply correlation [having a connection]. None of the previously conducted research has been able to determine if the brain differences, the poor elimination of toxins, the poor processing of proteins, and any of the other issues are causes or simply results of the autism.

What Do Allergies Have to Do with It?

The type of allergy that plays a role in autism is different than the allergies most people are aware of, such as reactions to bee stings. The kind of allergy associated with autism doesn't show up immediately; thus, you can more accurately refer to these allergies as intolerances to substances. Many autistic individuals are intolerant of dairy products or other common foods such as eggs. Some people believe that these intolerances wreak such havoc with the brain that they actually cause autism.

Others argue that anyone who's cured of autistic symptoms by reduced exposure to allergens was never autistic in the first place. Researchers have the proverbial chicken and egg problem here.

One theory, the *cerebral allergy theory*, points to how some intolerances are common across most of the autism spectrum. The theory states that the stomachs of some autistic people lack the enzymes needed to digest some proteins, and that these proteins cause harm to their brains by migrating into their bloodstreams (via leaky guts); the proteins may also cause the diarrhea or constipation common in autistic children. According to the Autism Society of America's "Statement on Dietary Interventions," research has found "elevated levels of certain peptides" in the urine of autistic children. . . .

Some parents who remove dairy products (containing casein) or wheat products (containing gluten), which are structurally similar proteins, report improvements in digestion, mood, and sleep. Some parents have claimed cures for their children through dietary and other interventions.

The maldigestion of dietary proteins theory also carries the label *opioid peptide theory*, because it seems that these proteins can act like opiates, or painkillers, in the systems of people who can't digest them.

Heavy-Metal Poisoning Hypotheses

If a child has too much metal in his or her system, it may be genetic or environmentally induced, or it may occur through an interaction between genetics and the environment. The problem is significant because high levels of these metals can disrupt the brain and the nervous system, resulting in autistic symptoms. Research done by neuropharmacologist Dr. Richard Deth, of Northeastern University, among others, is consistent with a heavy-metal theory of autism. . . . With this hypothesis, researchers state that a metal such as mercury or lead can cause neurodevelopmental disorders in a subset of susceptible children who lack the genetic ability to excrete heavy metals from their systems.

Some potential sources of mercury or other metals harmful to the body include the following:

- Dental amalgams or fillings
- Fish, such as tuna
- Power-plant emissions
- Lead-based paint
- Cigarette smoke

- Well or tap water
- Vaccines
- Swimming pools and hot tubs treated with copper sulfate

Some autistic children have been shown to have, when tested, excessively high levels of metals in their systems, although research has not yet established this as fact. Most healthy bodies excrete metals, but researchers have theorized that autistic children have great difficulty excreting them because of lower rates of glutathione and other proteins that work to eliminate metals such as aluminum, cadmium, lead, and mercury.

One subset of the heavy-metal theory proposes that pregnant women who ingest contaminated fish or have fillings containing mercury can pass the metals on to a developing fetus. However, it may not even be necessary for a child to gain exposure to higher-than-normal levels of a toxin—if he can't excrete metals from his system, even normal exposure may be problematic. Therefore, if a child has a heavy metal problem, doctors can't say for sure whether it's primarily an exposure problem or an excretion problem.

The heavy-metal pattern isn't identical in all cases. Many symptoms of autism are similar to the symptoms of heavy-metal poisoning. Although the symptoms of mercury poisoning and autism overlap by about 90 percent, some researchers have pointed out that the pattern of mercury poisoning is quite different from that of autism.

Autoimmune or Virus-Induced Theories of Causation

Anywhere from 30 to 70 percent of autistic children have subtle immune system abnormalities. Some doctors believe that autism may be triggered during pregnancy, due to environmental influences to the developing baby. Natural stress hormones from the mother, or any trauma such as chemical exposures, may disrupt normal early development.

Immune-system problems in a pregnant woman or developing child may also contribute to the symptoms, and maternal viral infections may be one of the noninherited causes. For example, epidemiological studies show a risk of autism in the offspring of mothers exposed to the rubella virus, or German measles, early in their pregnancies.

Many autistic individuals have family members with autoimmune diseases such as diabetes or rheumatoid arthritis, suggesting a link between autism and autoimmune problems. Certain research has suggested that a disruption in the balance of cytokines (protein molecules that carry messages between B, T, and other immune cells and that affect sleep and fever responses) is a possible cause of autism.

As you can see, some research suggests evidence for autoimmune theories, but other research is inconclusive. Autopsies of people with autism have revealed unusually low numbers of critical immune system signaling components, called *Purkinje cells*. However, research hasn't yet turned up a correlation between autoantibodies in the blood and brain abnormalities.

Causes of Asperger's Syndrome, an Autistic Spectrum Disorder

Tony Attwood

Tony Attwood, in the following selection, explains some of the causes of Asperger's syndrome. While it is part of the medical category of autism spectrum disorders, Asperger's syndrome individuals may have different causes for their disorder than do autistic individuals. As Attwood states, much recent research shows that the brain develops in a different way for people with Asperger's syndrome. Pregnancy complications and birth complications have also been associated with a significant number of individuals who developed Asperger's syndrome. According to the author further autism research may lead to the conclusive biological factors that cause Asperger's syndrome. Attwood, a psychologist, is the author of several books on Asperger's syndrome.

First of all, we know that Asperger's syndrome is not caused by inadequate parenting or psychological or physical trauma. Unfortunately, parents often think

SOURCE: Tony Attwood, *The Complete Guide to Asperger's Syndrome.* London, England: Jessica Kingsley Publishers, 2007. Copyright © Tony Attwood 2007. All rights reserved. Reproduced by permission of Jessica Kingsley Publishers.

the behaviour and profile of abilities are somehow caused by a defect in their own character or parenting skills, perhaps not providing enough love for the child; or some traumatic event such as witnessing an accident, or falling from a tree. Parents should abandon feelings of personal guilt. The research studies have clearly established that Asperger's syndrome is due to a dysfunction of specific structures and systems in the brain. In short, the brain is 'wired' differently, not necessarily defectively, and this was not caused by what a parent did or did not do during the child's development.

We are now able to conduct brain imaging studies of typical people that can identify the structures and systems

Medical testing can help to differentiate between autism and Asperger's syndrome, but little is known about how the diseases develop. **(AP Images.)**

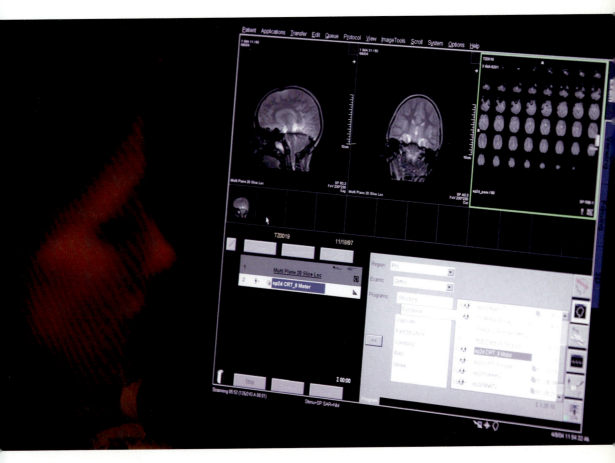

that operate together to form the 'social brain', and examine whether any of these structures function differently for people with Asperger's syndrome. Research studies that have used brain imaging technology and neuro-psychological tests have confirmed that Asperger's syndrome is associated with a dysfunction of the 'social brain', which comprises components of the frontal and temporal regions of the cortex—to be more precise, the medial prefrontal and orbitofrontal areas of the frontal lobes, the superior temporal sulcus, inferior basal temporal cortex, and temporal poles of the temporal lobes. There is also evidence of dysfunction of the amygdala, the basal ganglia and cerebellum. (Frith 2004; Gowen and Miall 2005; Toal, Murphy and Murphy 2005). The latest research suggests that there is weak connectivity between these components (Welchew *et al.* 2005). There is also evidence to suggest right hemisphere cortical dysfunction (Gunter *et al.* 2002) and an abnormality of the dopamine system (Nieminen-von Wendt *et al.* 2004). The neurological research examining brain function is consistent with the psychological profile of abilities in social reasoning, empathy, communication and cognition that are characteristics of Asperger's syndrome. Thus, we now know which structures in the brain are functioning or 'wired' differently.

But why did those areas of the brain develop differently? Probably for the majority of people with Asperger's syndrome, the reason is due to genetic factors. [Viennese physician Hans] Asperger originally noticed a ghosting or shadow of the syndrome in the parents (particularly fathers) of the children he saw, and proposed the condition could be inherited. Subsequent research has confirmed that for some families there are strikingly similar characteristics in family members. Research has indicated that, using strict diagnostic criteria for Asperger's syndrome, about 20 per cent of fathers and 5 per cent of mothers of a child with Asperger's syndrome have

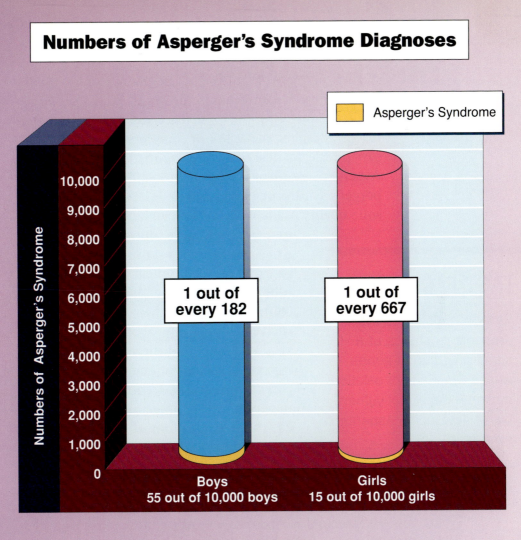

Numbers of Asperger's Syndrome Diagnoses

Asperger's Syndrome

Numbers of Asperger's Syndrome

10,000
9,000
8,000
7,000
6,000
5,000
4,000
3,000
2,000
1,000
0

1 out of every 182

1 out of every 667

Boys
55 out of 10,000 boys

Girls
15 out of 10,000 girls

Source: "What is the Epidemiology of Asperger's Disorder?" 2007. www.aspergers.com.

the syndrome themselves (Volkmar *et al.* 1998). While this information may not be a total surprise for their partner, they have usually not had a formal diagnosis. If one uses a broader description of Asperger's syndrome, almost 50 per cent of first-degree relatives of a child with Asperger's syndrome have similar characteristics (Bailey *et al.* 1998; Volkmar *et al.* 1998). When considering second- and third-degree relatives, more than two thirds of children with Asperger's syndrome have a relative with a similar pattern of abilities (Cederlund and Gillberg 2004). There is something in the genes. . . .

In Chapter 1 [of the *Complete Guide to Asperger's Syndrome*], I use the metaphor of completing a 100 piece jigsaw puzzle to describe the diagnostic assessment for Asperger's syndrome. Some pieces or aspects of Asperger's syndrome have a detrimental effect on the person's quality of life while others can be beneficial. Family members who have more of the characteristics of Asperger's syndrome than would be expected in a typical person may have inherited beneficial characteristics that contribute towards their success in careers such as engineering, accountancy and the arts. We know that there is a greater than expected number of engineers among the parents and grandparents of children with Asperger's syndrome (Baron Cohen *et al.* 2001b). The children of such individuals may then be at greater risk of having even more characteristics associated with Asperger's syndrome, such that there are sufficient [characteristics] for a diagnosis. The siblings of such a child will probably want to know the likely recurrence rate for Asperger's syndrome when they have their own children. At present, we have not identified the precise means of transmission or susceptibility genes but in the not-too-distant future, we may be able to identify the genetic transmission for a particular family.

A question often asked by the mother of a child with Asperger's syndrome is whether a difficult pregnancy or birth could have been the cause of the characteristics of Asperger's syndrome, or at least a contributory factor to the degree of expression. In Lorna Wing's (1981) original paper that first used the diagnostic term Asperger's syndrome, she noted that some of her cases had a history of pre-, peri- and post-natal [before, during, and after

> **FAST FACT**
>
> Research indicates the probable existence of a common group of genes whose variations or deletions make an individual vulnerable to developing Asperger's syndrome.

birth] conditions that could have caused cerebral (i.e. brain) dysfunction. Her original observation has been confirmed by subsequent studies. Pregnancy complications have been identified in 31 per cent of children with Asperger's syndrome, and peri-natal or birth complications in about 60 per cent (Cederlund and Gillberg 2004). However, no single complication during pregnancy or birth has been consistently identified as being associated with the later development of the signs of Asperger's syndrome. We also do not know if it was an already existing impairment in foetal development that subsequently affected obstetric events, with a difficult birth then increasing the degree of expression.

Children and Asperger's Syndrome

There does appear to be a greater incidence of babies who are small for gestational age, and marginally older mothers when the child was born (Cederlund and Gillberg 2004; Ghaziuddin, Shakal and Tsai 1995). There also appear to be more children with Asperger's syndrome than we would expect who were born either pre-term (36 weeks or less) or post-maturely (42 weeks or more) (Cederlund and Gillberg 2004). It is possible that factors that affect brain development during pregnancy and birth could affect the 'social brain' and contribute to the development of Asperger's syndrome.

Recent studies have indicated that for at least one in four children with Asperger's syndrome, their brain and head circumference grew at a faster rate than would be expected in the first few months after being born. The children developed macrocephalus or an unusually large head and brain (Cederlund and Gillberg 2004; Gillberg and de Souza 2002; Palmen *et al.* 2005). There may be two subgroups of children with Asperger's syndrome who have macrocephalus, one which includes children who had a large head at birth, and one which includes children who showed a rapid increase in brain size during early infancy. The initial acceleration eventually slows, so that in later childhood typical children have 'caught up', such that the differences in head circumference may not be so conspicuous when the child is about five years old. At the moment we do not have a satisfactory and proven explanation as to why this occurs. We know that brain enlargement can occur in young children with Asperger's syndrome and autism. There is also preliminary information to suggest that the frontal, temporal and parietal, but not the occipital, areas of the brain are enlarged, (Carper *et al.* 2002) and there is an increase in grey matter but not white matter (Palmen *et al.* 2005). Sometimes having a rapidly growing and relatively big brain, or at least parts of it, is not an advantage.

We recognize that Asperger's syndrome is part of the autism spectrum, and research on the aetiology or causes of autism may provide information on the causes of Asperger's syndrome. Thus, future research may indicate whether Asperger's syndrome could be caused by infections during pregnancy and in the child's early infancy, inborn errors of metabolism such that the digestion of specific foods produces toxins that affect brain development, or other biological factors that could affect brain development.

At present we cannot state with any certainty the specific cause of Asperger's syndrome in any child or adult, but at least we have some idea as to the possible causes, and know that parents can rest assured that it is not due to faulty parenting.

Treating Autism

Nancy D. Wiseman

In the following article Nancy Wiseman discusses the many treatment options available for individuals with autism. Several popular methods fall into three distinct categories: developmental approaches, behavioral approaches, and organizational approaches. As the author explains, each of these approaches focuses on a different aspect of autism. Developmental approaches focus on one-on-one time with an autistic child to help his or her overall emotional and social development. Behavioral approaches focus on teaching specific skills and behaviors. Organizational approaches focus on helping an autistic individual develop the best environment to maximize the ability to function and learn. The author also discusses several other therapies that can be used to help teach or improve the life of an autistic child or adult. Wiseman is the founder and president of First Signs, Inc., a national autism organization. She is also the mother of an autistic child.

SOURCE: Nancy D. Wiseman with Kim Painter Koffsky. *Could It Be Autism? A Parent's Guide to the First Signs and Next Steps,* New York, NY: Broadway Books, 2006. Copyright © 2006 by First Signs, Inc. All rights reserved. Used in the United States, its territories and possessions, Canada, P.I., Open Market, E.U. by permission of Broadway Books, a division of Random House, Inc. In the UK by permission of Lark Productions, LLC.

The cornerstone of initial treatment for many children with autism spectrum disorders, and sometimes for children with other delays and disorders, are therapies that rely on intense one-on-one interaction and/or a specially structured teaching environment. The most popular of these approaches fall into three categories: developmental, behavioral, and organizational.

Developmental Approaches

These focus on filling in a child's basic developmental gaps, rather than teaching specific language, academic, social, or other skills. Often these approaches start by connecting with the child emotionally and using that connection to engage him in ways that will move him up the developmental ladder. These approaches include:

DIR/Floortime

In this "developmental, individual-difference, relationship-based" approach, parents are trained to act as the primary therapists, literally getting down on the floor with their children, often for twenty- to thirty-minute periods, several times a day. By meeting the child at his developmental level and by following his lead, the parent attempts to engage him in increasingly longer and richer streams of back-and-forth communication and meaningful play. The therapy focuses on using the parent-child relationship as a building block for broader learning and emotional growth. The techniques also can be used by schools and by play, speech, and occupational therapists.

Relationship Development Intervention (RDI)

Parents also are the primary therapists in this approach, which starts by using a series of highly structured games and exercises to teach the child how to tune in to the actions and emotions of other people. The parent and child then move on to exercises that focus on back-and-forth communication, shared experiences and play, and, gradually, to less structured interactions that build social awareness and competence. Parents attend training sessions and also are supervised by therapists trained in the method.

Son-Rise

This method, taught by parents who helped a child overcome autism in the 1970s, emphasizes accepting the child and interacting with him in an enthusiastic, positive way, for many hours a day, in a specially designed home playroom. Parents and other therapists, who must attend training sessions, are encouraged to "join" the child in activities, like hand-flapping and repetitive play, that may be part of his disorder, but also to attempt to engage the child in more meaningful play and communication. No studies of this method have ever been published.

Behavioral Approaches

Based on a science called applied behavioral analysis (ABA), these methods focus on teaching the child specific skills and behaviors in a systematic, highly structured way, using constant rewards and repetition. The idea is to reinforce positive behavior (including all kinds of learning and appropriate social interaction) while reducing or eliminating behavior that gets in the way of learning and communicating. ABA programs often start with twenty-five to forty hours a week of therapy and can be conducted at home, at school, or both. As a child progresses, the program may become less structured and include more teaching during routine, daily activities.

Parents may be trained as therapists, but most home therapy is conducted by college students, supervised by more experienced behavioral specialists. Particular types of ABA include:

> **FAST FACT**
>
> Roughly 50 percent of children with autism who receive early intervention and intensive behavioral treatment can improve enough to succeed in school.

Discrete Trial Training (DTT)

This is the original and most structured form of ABA. A typical program for a child with classic autism might start by teaching the child how to sit in a chair and make eye contact and then proceed to teach language, academic, and social skills. Each skill is broken into small parts and taught in repetitive drills; therapists keep extensive data to track progress. The child is rewarded, often with bits of food, toys, or praise, for every appro-

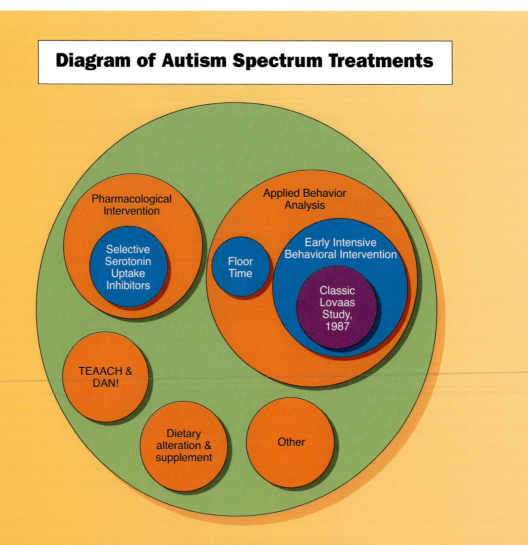

Diagram of Autism Spectrum Treatments

Pharmacological Intervention

Selective Serotonin Uptake Inhibitors

Applied Behavior Analysis

Floor Time

Early Intensive Behavioral Intervention

Classic Lovaas Study, 1987

TEAACH & DAN!

Dietary alteration & supplement

Other

Source: TIPOgen AS, 2005. www. tipogen.com.

priate response. Inappropriate responses are ignored or corrected.

Verbal Behavior (VB)

This variation of ABA focuses on teaching language by breaking it into small, functional parts that can be taught in a systematic way. A program starts by assessing the child's existing communication skills in minute detail. Then a curriculum is devised to fill in the gaps. A typical program for a child with classic autism might start by rewarding him for responding to his name or for imitating a sound, and then teach the child how to make requests, label objects, ask questions, follow increasingly complex directions, and, eventually, engage in conversation.

Organizational Approaches

These focus on creating a physical environment and routine that maximizes a person's ability to function and learn. The most common method:

Treatment and Education of Autistic and Related Communication-Handicapped Children (TEACCH)

This is primarily a classroom approach. It focuses on teaching children independent work and life skills, along with communication and social skills, and relies heavily on structured settings, predictable routines, and picture schedules—elements designed to build on the strengths and preferences of many children with autism spectrum disorders. Some parents also use elements of TEACCH at home.

In addition to these cornerstone approaches, most children with developmental delays and disorders receive a number of other therapies and treatments that fall into several [different] categories.

Clinical Therapies

These are directly provided by specially trained professionals.

Speech and Language Therapy

Therapists help children improve their ability to produce speech and use language. Some also help children improve eating skills. And some teach alternative forms of communication for children who cannot speak. Therapy can occur at school, at home, or in private offices, individually or in groups. The techniques used vary widely, depending on a child's diagnosis and developmental profile. A typical session might include mouth exercises and carefully targeted speaking and listening games.

Occupational Therapy

Children improve fine motor, self-help, and eating skills and may also work on sensory integration during group or individual sessions at home, at school, or in private offices. Techniques vary depending on the child's needs. During a typical session, a child might use swings, crawl through tunnels, and play with shaving cream, sand, clay, and other materials. She might also draw pictures, construct puzzles, and use scissors, zippers, buttons, eating utensils, and other common objects. School-age children may also work on handwriting.

Physical Therapy

The focus is on large motor skills, such as crawling or walking, jumping, running, and using playground equipment. Goals often include increased strength, balance, coordination, and mobility as well as better sensory integration. Services can be offered individually or in groups, at home, at school, or in private offices. Techniques vary depending on the child's needs, but a typical session might include physical exercises and games, as well as practice using stairs, play equipment, or other items in the child's everyday environment.

Auditory Integration Therapy

Children listen to a special selection of modified music or other sounds in an attempt to correct problems with processing and understanding speech and other sounds. Listening sessions are clustered together over a few days or weeks. This is a widely used but still experimental treatment.

Vision Therapy

Exercises and sometimes special lenses are designed to retrain the visual system—the eyes and key brain areas—in children who have trouble seeing or trouble understanding and learning from what they see. This method, also known as eye training, behavioral optometry, or orthoptic therapy, is sometimes described as "physical therapy for the eyes."

Biomedical Treatments

Medications

Prescription drugs can be used to treat some symptoms, including hyperactivity, anxiety, tics, and mood instability, as well as accompanying disorders, such as seizures, allergies, and gastrointestinal problems. Many of the medications can have serious side effects, so their risks must be weighed carefully against potential benefits. Doses should also be kept as low as possible. Often, many different drugs are available to treat the same symptoms or conditions, so the best choices must be found through trial and error.

Chelation

Compounds taken by mouth, IV, or rubbed on the skin can be used to reduce toxic levels of heavy metals, such as lead and mercury, in the child's body. Some of the compounds carry a risk of liver damage and can cause or worsen gastrointestinal and behavioral problems. The creams generally have a foul odor as well.

This is an experimental treatment for children with autism spectrum disorders, based on the theory that an overload of heavy metals, especially mercury, contributes to physical and behavioral symptoms.

Diet

Special food plans, including some that eliminate certain food groups, can be used to treat metabolic conditions, prevent allergic reactions, relieve gastrointestinal symptoms, or optimize nutrition. Dietary changes may also improve learning and behavior in some children, though this has yet to be proven in carefully controlled studies.

Vitamins and Supplements

Some doctors and nutritionists advise larger-than-usual amounts of certain vitamins and other nutrients for children with particular developmental and health profiles. The effectiveness of these substances is generally unproven, except in some rare disorders. Children should not take high-dose vitamins and supplements except under medical supervision.

Immunological Treatments

Therapies that can alter the immune system, including steroids and infusions of intravenous immunoglobulin (IVIG), are used to treat confirmed or suspected immunological deficits in some children. These treatments, which carry long-term health risks, are sometimes used in language-impaired children with certain kinds of seizures. Their use in other conditions is under study.

Secretin

This hormone has been reported to help some individual children with autism, but clinical studies, comparing secretin to placebos, have failed to show a benefit.

Additional Therapies

Augmentative Communication

Alternative forms of communication, which can include picture cards (such as picture exchange communication [PEC]), sign language (including American Sign Language), letter boards, and computerized devices, are used as primary, long-term communication strategies or as bridges to oral language.

Rapid-Prompting Method

In this technique, developed by the mother of a nonverbal young man with severe autism, a teacher uses rapid speech and other intense stimuli to keep the attention of a student and to prompt rapid responses from him. The idea is to teach students to respond by pointing to choices on a letter board or piece of paper. This technique has undergone no scientific study.

Facilitated Communication

In this controversial technique, a nonverbal person types on a computer keyboard while someone else supports his hand or arm. Several studies strongly suggest that in many cases, the thoughts communicated are those of the facilitator, not the disabled person. However, some individuals who start typing with a facilitator later type—and apparently communicate—on their own.

Music Therapy

A music therapist, working with children individually or in groups, can use singing, movement, and instrument play to work on language, communication, social, motor, and sensory issues.

Animal Therapy

Children, often guided by occupational therapists, interact with animals (often horses or dolphins) to work on sensory and motor issues and to build confidence. Some children also work with dogs and other pets to build relationship skills.

Play Therapy

A professional—often a social worker, a psychologist, or a speech therapist—engages the child in play to work on emotional issues, communication, and social skills.

Laughter and social skills can be critical to an autistic child developing normal relationships with the outside world. (AP Images.)

Therapists work with children individually or in groups and may employ techniques also used in Floortime, psychotherapy, or speech and language therapy.

Recreational Therapy

Participation in swimming, gymnastics, dance, art, and other activities (sometimes adapted for children with special needs) is recommended for some children. Many communities also offer summer camps for children with special needs.

Social Stories

Simple stories, composed with pictures and, sometimes words, are used to teach children social and self-help skills and to prepare them for changes in routine and new situations, from vacations to shopping trips. Parents and teachers can buy books containing basic social stories, but usually learn to write their own to meet the child's individual needs.

Social Skills Groups

Children get together to work on social and play skills, in groups overseen by a psychologist, social worker, or other professional participants. They learn the rules of social interaction and are trained to recognize and read social cues, show appropriate interest in others, and recognize and correct their own socially inappropriate behaviors.

CHAPTER 2

The Controversial Side of Autism

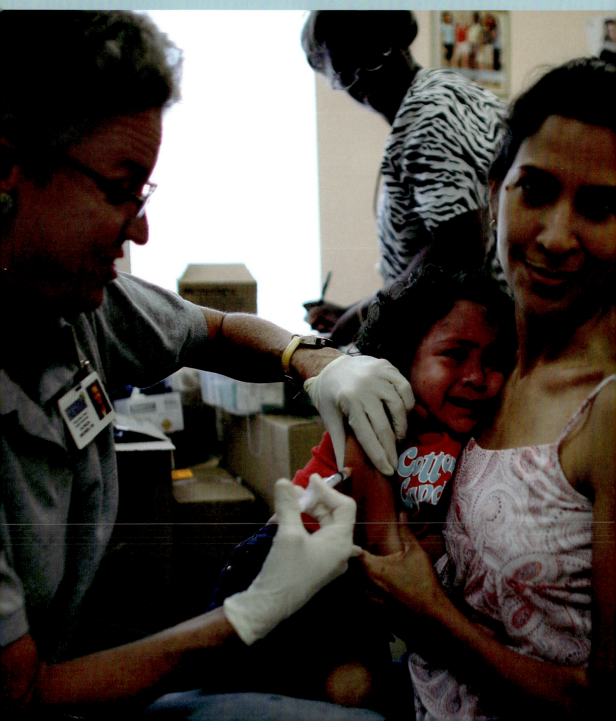

Vaccines May Cause Autism

The Autism Society of America

In the following selection the Autism Society of America argues that a very strong relationship exists between vaccines and rates of autism. The society believes that this is due to the use of thimerosal, a mercury-based preservative, in the vaccines. According to the Autism Society, since a causal link between mercury in vaccines and autism has not been disproven, vaccines containing thimerosal should no longer be available. Since autism cases are rising in unprecedented numbers, more research dollars should be spent and different research avenues explored in the search to understand and conquer this disorder. The Autism Society of America has begun a program to advance autism research and help facilitate collaborative research efforts of different programs. This national organization focuses on raising public awareness of the disorder and helping individuals and families cope with the everyday aspects of autism.

Photo on facing page.
The relationship between vaccines and autism is hotly debated.
(Getty Images)

SOURCE: The Autism Society of America, "Written Statement for the Record of The Autism Society of America to the U.S. House of Representatives Committee on Appropriations, Subcommittee on Labor, Health and Human Services, Education, and Related Agencies: Influenza Vaccine," The Autism Society of America, October 5, 2004. Reproduced by permission.

A utism is the fastest growing disability in this nation today. What does that mean? . . .

- Over the 1990's, our U.S. population grew at 13%, while non-autism disabilities grew at 28.4%.

- Autism grew at the rate of 1,354%.

- Today 3 out of every 500 newborn babies will likely have autism, a jump from 2 in 500 births that ASA [Autism Society of America] published just two years ago [in 2002]. That means that more than 60 families will likely receive a diagnosis of autism today alone.

- ASA estimates that the annual cost of autism to the U.S. economy is as much as $90 billion for services,

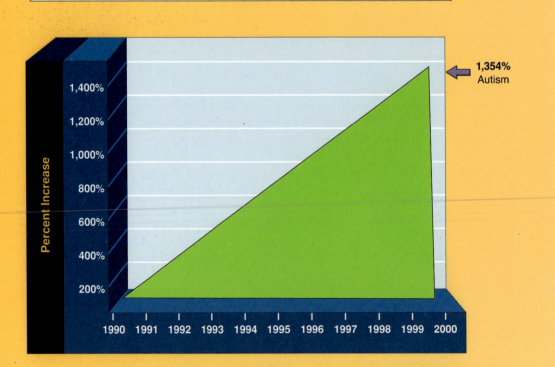

Increase in Autism Diagnoses, 1990–2000

1,354%
Autism

Source: Autism Society of America, 2004.

treatment and related costs. At historical rates of growth, this could escalate over the next decade to more than $300 billion annually.

As you may recall, on April 18, 2002, [ASA president] Lee Grossman presented the following testimony to the House Committee on Government Reform:

> The only way to prevent this economic fallout from becoming a reality is to invest more money in research to solve the puzzle of autism, to expand educational and vocational opportunities, and to create support services that are currently lacking or non-existent for those already affected by autism.

Mr. Chairman, while much progress has been made over the past 2 years, the above statement holds true. Clearly our Nation is still facing a public health crisis of epidemic proportions. . . .

It is vital that our government commit sufficient resource to deal with the autism epidemic.

State of Autism Research Related to Vaccine Injury

ASA firmly believes that research must continue into the possible association between vaccines and neurodevelopmental disabilities. Until more definitive answers are available to questions dealing with the etiology of autism spectrum disorders, continuing this research just makes good scientific sense. ASA has repeatedly sought to ensure that the federal government support necessary research and fund the biological and clinical research needed to get at the facts. Further, until more is known as to the cause or causes of autism, we must take steps to eliminate potential risk factors, such as reducing mercury exposure to pregnant mothers, fetuses and newborns. Again, this just makes good scientific sense. Toxicologists involved in mercury research have repeatedly testified to Congress and government bodies that mercury in all of its forms, including ethylmercury/thimerosal is a potent neurotoxin.

During the 1990s, millions of infants and toddlers were exposed to mercury above federal guidelines because of a rising number of routine shots in which thimerosal was a common ingredient used to prevent bacterial contamination. Since 1999, the chemical has been reduced, but not eliminated. Vaccine makers and many health officials say there is no proof of a causal link between thimerosal and autism. To which ASA adds that there is no definitive proof there is not a causal link. The question remains open.

FAST FACT

Data from a 2006 study shows that since mercury was removed from childhood vaccines, the reported rates of autism and other neurological disorders in children not only stopped increasing but actually dropped sharply —by as much as 35 percent.

Given the increasing concerns about mercury exposures and our ability to eliminate this particular exposure, HR 4169 completes actions begun five years ago to ban mercury from vaccines. "[The] Public Health Service, the American Academy of Pediatrics, and vaccine manufacturers agree that thimerosal-containing vaccines should be removed as soon as possible," stated the proclamation issued in July 1999. Yet five years later thimerosal—50% mercury—remains in some nonroutine childhood vaccines. The government is recommending the flu vaccine be given to infants and pregnant women without stating a preference for the mercury-free version of the inoculation.

When to Vaccinate

Of additional concern to ASA is the need to further understand when to vaccinate children with known allergies and seizure disorders. A significant portion of the autism population also deal with seizure disorders or allergies. Both of these issues present difficult choices for parents who want to protect against infectious diseases such as influenza, but for which immunizations may pose an additional risk. ASA fully supports recommendations for research to further understand these areas of vaccine safety. These issues are important to both the pediatric and adult autism populations.

H.R. 4169—The Mercury Free Vaccines Act of 2004

On April 2 [2004], Rep. Dave Weldon introduced along with Rep. Carolyn Maloney, H.R. 4169—The Mercury Free Vaccines Act of 2004. . . . H.R. 4169 will phase-out the use of mercury in vaccines over the next 3 years, giving particular attention to completely eliminating mercury from childhood vaccines on an expedited schedule. This bill is in response to the fact that:

- The safety of thimerosal in vaccines is not proven;

- Mercury is well-established as a neurotoxin;

- According to the EPA 1 in 6 newborns is born with a blood mercury level considered unsafe;

- The FDA and the EPA recently warned pregnant women, nursing mothers, and young children to limit their consumption of certain fish that are high in mercury;

- No one at the NIH or CDC can tell you what happens to the mercury once injected into an infant—Where does it go? How much goes to critical organs? How much to the brain? Can it cause damage to the developing central nervous system?

No one can answer these questions and these uncertainties should be resolved before pregnant women and infants are exposed to more mercury. Relevant federal agencies are reversing their position of precaution of the past five years by adopting a policy reintroducing mercury into childhood vaccines by recommending the flu vaccine, most of which contain mercury, for infants at 6, 7, and 23 months of age. Vaccines can be, and are, made without mercury, so why not remove the mercury and remove any doubt? After five years this should be a [moot] point. The mercury should be out of all vaccines to which children and the unborn are exposed to.

States Introduce Thimerosal Legislation

Across our nation, several states have come forward with legislation eliminating thimerosal. Recently, California became the second state to ban thimerosal in certain vaccinations given to pregnant women and young children. Iowa was the first. In a signing message, Gov. Schwarzenegger [California] noted that although the best available evidence finds no link between thimerosal and autism, the U.S. Food and Drug Administration and the American Academy of Pediatrics in 1999 recommended the removal of thimerosal from childhood vaccines.

"I believe that an abundance of caution merits the acceleration of the process already underway to remove

Some believe that vaccines containing thimerosal may be causing the increase in autism diagnoses. (AP Images.)

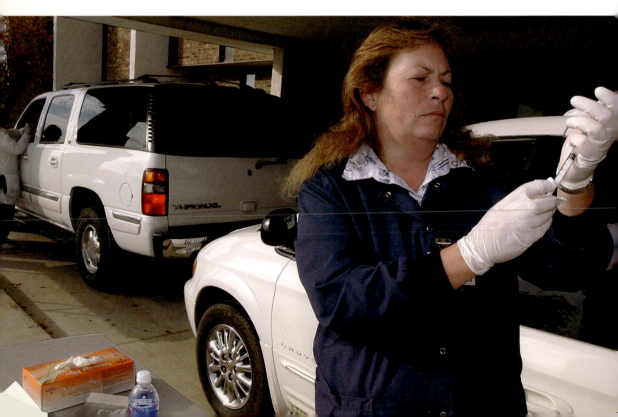

thimerosal from the last few vaccines that contain it, as intended by AB 2943," Schwarzenegger wrote.

ASA agrees. Any time we can reduce public exposure to mercury and other known neurotoxins, we should do so.

Biomedical Interventions for Autism

On October 22–23 [2004], ASA joins the Indiana Autism Resource Center to sponsor "Racing Towards Answers in Autism," a comprehensive conference to look at the latest in biomedical interventions specific to autism spectrum disorders. . . .

Our goal is to foster additional collaborative research between practice-based research programs, academia and colleagues throughout HHS [U.S. Department of Health and Human Services]. By creating a forum for the dialogue on topics ranging from genetics to immune related disorders, we hope to meld together the leading research into a more focused application of clinical interventions. Our intent, is to have the attendees not only learn the latest in biomedical research, but be able to take this information and make an immediate impact on the lives of those on the autism spectrum.

For the subset of the Autism community and ASA membership who are dealing with a dual diagnosis of autism and mercury poisoning or mercury toxicity, these types of programs are key in looking for opportunities to develop safe and effective therapeutic interventions for the mercury body burden. Practice-based Research is showing that for children whose mercury burden is addressed early and effectively that some of the symptoms associated with autism dissipate. These areas of therapeutic intervention need more focus and research funding. . . .

Autism, today, is a disability of epidemic proportion, affecting everyone in this nation. Please help us ensure that all affected by autism and their families are provided every opportunity for a full and productive life.

No Link Exists Between Vaccines and Autism

Michelle Meadows

The U.S. Food and Drug Administration (FDA) argues in the following viewpoint that no association connects the use of vaccines and autism. The FDA states that the Institute of Medicine's Immunization Safety Review Committee has done studies on the link between vaccines and autism. Several concerns were addressed including potential biological links between autism and vaccines. According to the FDA eliminating the use of thimerosal was recommended as a precautionary measure to address public concern, even though no connection has been shown between vaccines and the development of autism. Vaccines should not be changed in any way, according to the author.

The U.S. Food and Drug Administration is part of the U.S. Department of Health and Human Services and oversees the quality and production of food and medicines in the United States. Meadows writes for *FDA Consumer* magazine.

SOURCE: Michelle Meadows, "IOM Report: No Link Between Vaccines and Autism," FDA Consumer, September–October 2004.

There is no link between autism and the measles-mumps-rubella (MMR) vaccine or the vaccine preservative thimerosal, according to a report released by the Institute of Medicine's (IOM) Immunization Safety Review Committee. [The IOM is part of the National Academy of Sciences.]

The report, released in May 2004, was prepared by a committee of independent experts established by the IOM in 2001 at the request of the Centers for Disease Control and Prevention (CDC) and the National Institutes of Health (NIH) to evaluate evidence on potential links between childhood vaccines and health problems. The agencies explored the issue because of growing controversy and questions from the public about vaccine safety.

Some parents have expressed concern because the symptoms of autism typically emerge in a child's second year of life, around the same time children first receive the MMR vaccine. Autism is a complex set of severe developmental disorders characterized by repetitive behavior and impaired social interaction and communication abilities. Other concerns the committee looked at include the use of thimerosal, a mercury-based compound used as a vaccine preservative, because many forms of mercury are known to damage the nervous system in high doses.

No Association Between Autism and MMR Vaccines

This latest IOM report follows two reports on vaccines and autism published in 2001. The committee determined then that the evidence did not show an association between the MMR vaccine and autism, but that more evidence was needed regarding thimerosal. "The committee concluded that the evidence available at that time was inadequate to accept or reject a causal relationship between thimerosal and neurodevelopmental disorders," says Marie McCormick, M.D., Sc.D., chairwoman

No Link Between MMR and Autism

This graph shows the results of a 2005 study in Yokohama, Japan, that indicates that the measles, mumps, and rubella (MMR) vaccine does not cause autism.

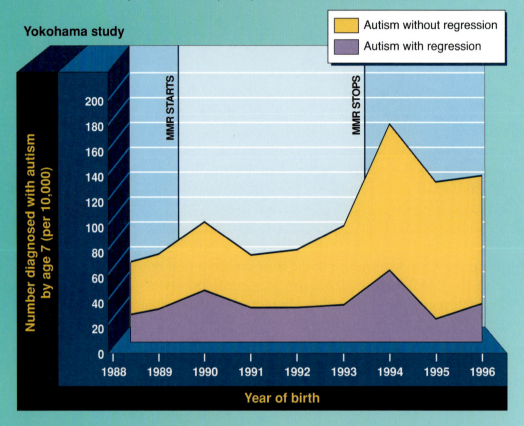

Yokohama study

Legend:
- Autism without regression
- Autism with regression

MMR STARTS

MMR STOPS

Y-axis: Number diagnosed with autism by age 7 (per 10,000) — 0, 20, 40, 60, 80, 100, 120, 140, 160, 180, 200

X-axis (Year of birth): 1988, 1989, 1990, 1991, 1992, 1993, 1994, 1995, 1996

Source: Andy Coghlan, "Autism Rises Despite MMR Ban in Japan," March 3, 2005. www.newscientist.com.

of the immunization safety committee and a professor at the Harvard School of Public Health.

The committee revisited these issues because several studies exploring possible links between vaccines and autism have been published since 2001. Committee members concluded that the hypothesis about how the MMR vaccine and thimerosal could trigger autism lacks supporting evidence. Their conclusions were based on a careful review of well-designed studies and other information from researchers and parents.

Five large studies in the United States, the United Kingdom, Denmark, and Sweden done since 2001 found no evidence of a link between autism and vaccines containing thimerosal. And 14 large studies consistently showed no link between the MMR vaccine and autism.

The committee also reviewed several studies that did report associations between vaccines and autism and found that these studies had limitations and lacked supporting evidence.

Biological Links Not a Concern

The committee reviewed potential biological links between vaccines and autism and found them to be only theoretical. Examples of some of the hypothesized links include a suggestion that the measles virus in the MMR vaccine might lodge in the intestines and trigger the release of toxins that could lead to autism. Another hypothesis is that the MMR vaccine might stimulate the release of immune factors that damage the central nervous system. Yet another hypothesis is that thimerosal may interfere with biochemical systems in the brain, thereby causing autism. But according to the IOM report, no evidence has shown that the immune system or its activation play a direct role in causing autism, and autism has not been documented as being a result of exposure to high doses of mercury.

> **FAST FACT**
>
> In a wide-ranging study conducted in Denmark between 1991 and 1998, researchers concluded that the risk of autism was the same in vaccinated children as it was in unvaccinated children.

"There is no convincing evidence of serious harm from the low doses of thimerosal in vaccines," says Karen Midthun, M.D., deputy director for medicine in the FDA's Center for Biologics Evaluation and Research (CBER). CBER regulates vaccines in the United States and works with the CDC and the NIH to study and monitor vaccine safety and effectiveness.

Limiting Thimerosal Use

Since the 1930s, small amounts of thimerosal have been used as a preservative in multi-dose vials of vaccines to prevent bacterial contamination. The active ingredient in thimerosal is ethylmercury.

Even though the risk of thimerosal is hypothetical, thimerosal began to be removed from childhood vaccines in 1999. The federal government, the American

New Jersey assemblyman Louis Greenwald, center, receives a hepatitis B vaccine injection at a press conference. Federal research has indicated that the link between vaccines and the increase in autistic patients is negligible. (AP Images.)

Academy of Pediatrics, and others agreed that thimerosal should be reduced and eliminated in vaccines as a precautionary measure. The FDA encouraged companies to comply with this recommendation. Currently, all routinely recommended vaccines manufactured for infants in the United States are either thimerosal-free or contain only trace amounts.

"We moved in this direction to address public concern and because it was feasible to eliminate mercury from vaccines," Midthun says. "We could eliminate thimerosal in vaccines as a way to reduce a child's total exposure to mercury, whereas other environmental sources of exposure are more difficult to eliminate."

In its latest report, the IOM's immunization committee reported that it does not dispute that mercury-containing compounds, including thimerosal, can be damaging to the nervous system. But the committee did not find that these damaging effects are related to the development of autism. . . .

Flu Vaccines

The CDC is recommending that children ages 6 months to 23 months get vaccinated annually against the flu (influenza) with the inactivated flu shot.

"The influenza vaccine is available both with thimerosal as a preservative and without it," Midthun says. "But the benefits of flu vaccination outweigh any theoretical risk from thimerosal."

According to the CDC, the amount of flu vaccine without thimerosal as a preservative will increase as manufacturing capabilities expand. "To eliminate thimerosal as a preservative from flu vaccines, manufacturers will have to switch from multi-dose to single-dose preparations, which requires greater filling and storage capacity," Midthun says.

Based on federal guidelines on levels of mercury exposure, a child won't receive excessive mercury from vaccines, regardless of whether their inoculation against the flu contains thimerosal.

No Immunization Changes

The IOM's immunization safety committee did not recommend any changes with the MMR vaccine or with the current schedule of routine childhood immunizations.

"While the committee strongly supports research that focuses on achieving a better understanding of autism, we recommend that future research be directed toward other lines of inquiry that are supported by current knowledge and evidence, and that offer more promise for finding an answer," McCormick said at a media briefing. "Given the current evidence, the vaccine hypothesis doesn't offer that promise."

Older Fathers Risk Having Autistic Children

Shankar Vedantam

In the following article Shankar Vedantam contends that children with older fathers are more likely to develop autism. According to the author the risk of autism rises as a father ages. Fathers in their forties have a much higher risk of having an autistic child and this risk increases even more for fathers in their fifties. A study of Israeli children shows an overall connection between older fathers and the incidence of autistic children. Vedantam is a staff writer for the *Washington Post*, covering many topics including medicine and health.

Children born to fathers of advancing age are at significantly higher risk of developing autism compared with children born to younger fathers, according to a comprehensive study published yesterday that offers surprising new insight into one of the most feared disorders of the brain.

The finding comes at a time of great controversy over autism in the United States, as a recent surge in diagnoses has fueled speculations about various possible causes of the disorder. For scientists, both the origins of and potential treatments for the disorder remain a mystery.

Risk Grows as a Father Ages

With every decade of advancing age starting with men in their teens and twenties, the new study found, older fathers pose a growing risk to their children when it comes to autism—unhappy evidence that the medical risks associated with late parenthood are not just the province of older mothers, as much previous research has suggested.

Of special concern is the finding that the risk for autism not only increases with paternal age but also appears to accelerate.

When fathers are in their thirties, children have about 1 1/2 times the risk of developing autism of children of fathers in their teens and twenties. Compared with the offspring of the youngest fathers, children of fathers in their forties have more than five times the risk of developing autism, and children of fathers in their fifties have more than nine times the risk.

Autism is a developmental disorder that is often characterized by social and verbal problems. It becomes manifest early in childhood and is associated with learning deficits and other problems. Many cases are diagnosed shortly after children enter school, where differences among kids become too obvious to ignore.

A wide variety of interventions are increasingly available for autistic children, and early behavioral interventions have been said to help with outcomes and functioning. There is, however, no cure for the disorder, and scientists are not sure about its biological roots.

FAST FACT

As men age, their genetic material repairs itself less effectively, and spontaneous genetic mutations may get passed on instead of corrected.

Autism Risk with Older Fathers

This chart reflects the 2006 findings of a study done in Israel that indicates that older fathers have a higher risk of having children with autism.

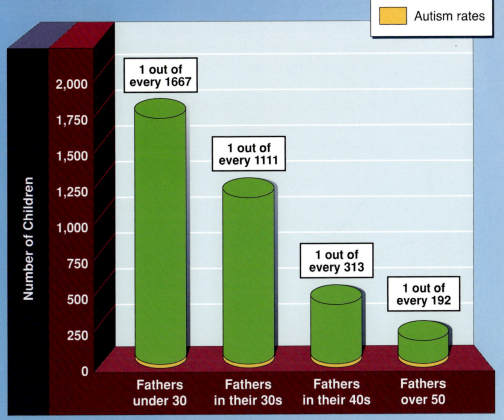

Source: Shankar Vedantam, "Autism Risk Rises with Age of Father," *Washington Post*, September 5, 2006.

378,891 People Are Analyzed

The new study presents an intriguing new avenue for research, because it suggests that genetic traits passed along by fathers, as opposed to mothers, may play some significant role in creating susceptibility to autism. Several other studies have suggested that older parents of both sexes are at greater risk of having children with developmental disorders. Three earlier studies looking at the relationship between paternal age and autism have produced mixed results; the new study is the most rigorous analysis conducted to date.

The study was based on an enormous sample of 17-year-olds—nearly all the male and three-quarters of the female subjects of that age found over a six-year period in Israel, as they came of draft age. In all, data from 378,891 people were analyzed.

Since all Israeli citizens have a unique identification number, and the draft process routinely calls for listing the identification numbers of parents, researchers were able to develop a large-scale map that allowed them to

Research has shown that a father's age can affect the probability of having an autistic child. (Associated Press)

determine the age of both parents for 132,271 draft candidates. They then compared that information against medical evaluations conducted by the draft board for autism and other disorders for those same candidates.

Important Link Between Autism and a Father's Age

Abraham Reichenberg at the Mount Sinai School of Medicine in New York, along with several others at research institutions in the United States and Israel, found a significant relationship between paternal age and autism, even after accounting for other factors, such as mothers' age and socioeconomic status.

Children of fathers who were 15 to 29 years of age had a risk of about six in 10,000 of developing autism. Children of fathers in their thirties had a risk of nine in 10,000. Children of fathers in their forties had a risk of 32 in 10,000, and children of fathers who were older than 50 had a risk of 52 in 10,000.

In a paper published yesterday [September 4, 2006] in the *Archives of General Psychiatry*, the researchers said that the number of cases of autism among families with the oldest dads was too small to lead to definitive conclusions about that group, but that there was little doubt about the overall trend. The only question, they said, is whether the risk accumulates at an accelerating rate with advancing paternal age, as the numbers in this study suggest.

Autism in General on the Rise?

Scientists in the United States are increasingly thinking about autism in terms of a spectrum of problems, which is why they have coined the term "autism spectrum disorders."

The federal government estimates that the risk for autism spectrum disorders in the United States is around 3.4 for every 1,000 children between the ages of 3 and 10.

Whether that number is on the rise has been hotly contested; better outreach and diagnostic efforts may be finding children who would previously have gone undetected. Enduring disparities in access to health care complicate the picture. While the medical complexities of autism are present in Israel, concern over disparities is mitigated to some extent because Israel has universal health insurance, which guarantees equal access to care.

The Israeli military draft board's medical diagnostic system does not differentiate among conditions on the autism spectrum, which includes autism, Asperger's syndrome, Rett syndrome and what are known as pervasive developmental disorders.

Autistic people can be unresponsive in social situations, or focused intently on a single task or object for long periods. While some parents recognize that their babies seem different from a very young age, U.S. government researchers also say that sometimes engaging and babbling babies can suddenly turn "silent, withdrawn, self-abusive, or indifferent to social overtures."

In recent years, concern and controversy have grown —despite a lack of conclusive evidence—that mercury in children's vaccines produces toxicity that leads to autism.

While the link between older fathers and autistic children is likely to be genetic, the researchers who conducted the new study also acknowledged the possibility that unknown other factors could simultaneously be causing men to delay parenthood while independently increasing autism rates.

Older Fathers Do Not Show Increased Risk of Having Autistic Children

Child Health Alert

In the following viewpoint, Child Health Alert discusses the finding of an Israeli study that showed and increased risk of autism for children with older fathers. According to Child Health Alert, the findings of this study must be kept in perspective. While there appears to be a link between the age of the father and the incidence of autism, the authors assert that this link does not necessarily mean that a father's advanced age is a cause of autism. Furthermore, the authors explain that even among the children of older fathers, the risk fo autism is still extremely small. Child Health Alert is an organization focusing on the health and well-being of children by helping adults understand issues in the news that affect children.

Autism is a developmental disorder that has become the focus of great attention in recent years, partly because the number of autistic children has been increasing dramatically. Older mothers and fathers

SOURCE: Child Health Alert, "Is a Child's Autism Related to His Father's Age?" *Child Health Alert*, vol. 24, October 2006, pp. 1–2. Copyright 2006 Child Health Alert Inc. Reproduced by permission.

have been linked to an increased risk of neurodevelopmental disorders in their children, so researchers conducted a study to see if parents' age was related to autism.

The authors studied people born during the 1980s in Israel, where at age 17 boys and the large majority of girls are required to register for the military draft. Draft records include information on many factors, including the medical conditions of the teenagers and their parents' ages. In a group of over 130,000 records that had complete information available, there were 100 cases listed as "autistic spectrum disorder" (ASD), and these were mainly cases of autism. Among children born to fathers under the age of 30, 6 per 10,000 had ASD, whereas among children born to fathers in their 40s, the rate was 31 per 10,000.

After taking into account a number of factors, including the age of the mothers, the authors found that chil-

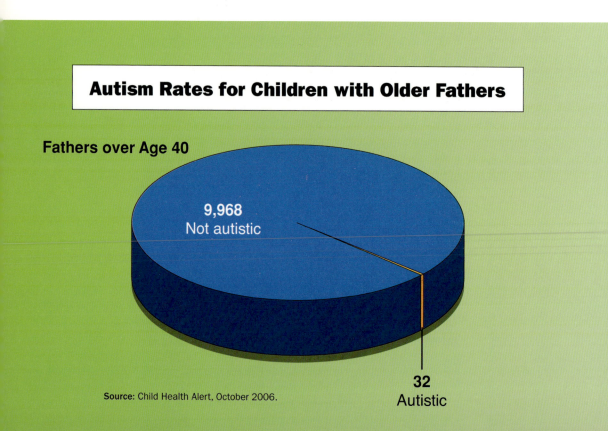

Autism Rates for Children with Older Fathers

Fathers over Age 40

9,968
Not autistic

32
Autistic

Source: Child Health Alert, October 2006.

Children born to men forty years or older are almost six times more likely to have autism then children born to men under thirty. (**Associated Press**)

dren born to men 40 years or older were almost 6 times more likely to have ASD than were children born to men under the age of 30 years. They conclude that "advanced paternal age was associated with increased risk of ASD," and suggest this could be the result of various factors related to aging or genetics. [Reichenberg *et al*].

Keeping Statistics in Perspective

Not surprisingly, this report made the news, and with all the controversy about autism these days, it may be hard to place this report in perspective. On the one hand, rates of autism have increased as parents have become older, so it might make sense that parents' age (in this case, the father's age) might be related to the increase in autism. However, other things have also been going on during the time that reports of autism have been increasing. For example, we've become much more sensitive to autism in recent years, and more and more children who might not have been diagnosed some years ago are now coming to attention.

FAST FACT

Almost six times as many boys as girls develop autism. When the fathers are over 40, the ratio is 1 to 1.

Even if the authors are correct that autism is linked to older fathers, that link doesn't mean that being an older father actually caused the autism. And even if being an older father actually did cause autism, remarkably few children born to older fathers were at risk. This study found that autism was almost 6 times more common among children born to older fathers, but it's important to keep in mind that among these older fathers, the risk of autism was only 32 per 10,000 children—or put another way, 9,968 children out of 10,000 (over 99%) did NOT have autism.

What does all this mean? First, if fathers' age increases the risk of autism, it has very little impact, overall, on that risk. Second, this study seems to reinforce the unfortunate reality that we have a long way to go before we can figure out what factors are accounting for the large number of autism cases we are seeing these days.

Specific Diets Can Help Treat Autism

Bruce Semon

Bruce Semon states in this viewpoint that too much *Candida albicans* yeast in the gastrointestinal tract can cause autistic behavior to worsen. This yeast is responsible for slowing down the brain and nervous system. By using an anti-yeast medication, autism patients often show noticeable improvements in the areas of speech, behavior, and sleep patterns. A gluten-free and casein-free diet, according to Semon, can also greatly reduce the symptoms of autism.

Finally, Semon says that using the gastrointestinal tract as a barometer of what is going on in the body is very helpful since many individuals with autism also suffer from stomach and intestinal problems. Semon has a doctorate in nutrition, is a child psychiatrist, and is the parent of an autistic child.

Autistic disorder is a severe developmental disorder, which was first described around 1940, about three years after the introduction of the first

SOURCE: Bruce Semon, "Autism: You Can Help by Changing to a Yeast Free, Gluten Free, Casein Free Diet and Using Homeopathy," www.ei-resource.org, 2004. Reprinted with permission of Dr. Bruce Semon, M.D., Ph.D, and www.nutritioninstitute.com/Autism.html.

major commercial antibiotics, the sulfa drugs. As antibiotic usage grows, so do rates of autism. Autistic disorder is a disorder of the antibiotic era. Why? Because antibiotics help the yeast *Candida albicans* grow in the intestinal tract. *Candida albicans* makes toxic chemicals which hurt the developing brain.

The yeast *Candida albicans* can be found inside of our intestinal tract, mouth and in the female genital tract. Sometimes this yeast overgrows and the doctor recognizes this overgrowth of yeast as a yeast infection of the female genital tract or in the mouth, where this infection is commonly called thrush.

Bacteria are also resident inside the intestinal tract, sharing space with the yeast. Antibiotics kill bacteria, not yeast. After the use of antibiotics the yeast grow to fill in the space left by the removal of the bacteria. Yeast make chemicals which kill bacteria, which enables the

Results of a Gluten-Free Casein-Free Diet

Results			
Quality	Percentage	Respondent's average age at diet start	Average time spent on diet
Dramatic	11.5% (16)	3.0 years	18 months
Excellent	29.5% (42)	3.3 years	13 months
Good	27% (37)	4.7 years	8 months
Moderate	22.6% (31)	4.4 years	7 months
No Result	5% (7)	5.7 years	1 month
Regression	4.4% (6)	5.5 years	7 months

Source: "The GFCF Diet." www.gfcfdiet.com.

yeast to grow at a higher level, even after the antibiotics have been stopped.

Chemical Compounds from Yeast

Yeast make a number of chemical compounds which are then picked up and absorbed into the body. These compounds are quite toxic to the nervous system. These compounds include toxic alcohols and acetone, as well as the powerful nervous system poison hydrogen sulfide. Alcohols depress and slow the nervous system and acetone causes coma. These chemicals slow the brain down so that the brain no longer works correctly. These chemicals should be cleared by the liver so that these chemicals never reach the brain. However in some people, these chemicals are apparently not cleared, reach the brain, and cause mental symptoms.

> **FAST FACT**
>
> According to surveys, as many as 40 percent of children with autism have been placed on special diets.

Slowing of the brain, especially in speech areas has been found in brains of autistic children. Alcohols are well known to disrupt brain development.

There are also chemicals in the diet which slow the brain down. Barley malt, the raw material for making beer, contains twenty chemicals which slow the brain down. Vinegar also contains such chemicals.

The combination of chemicals from internal yeast and from food could partially account for the finding of the brain slowing in autistic children.

Treating the Yeast Problem

The important reason to look at yeast as a major contributor to autism causation is that yeast is easily and safely treatable.

The way to reverse this yeast problem is to take the anti-yeast drug nystatin. This drug is not absorbed and kills the yeast living in the intestinal tract. Then the yeast can no longer make the toxic chemical compounds. Second, the diet contains many foods which contain yeast compounds. Some of these yeast chemicals are toxic to bacteria and will clear space for the yeast to grow again. If these yeast chemicals are left in the diet, nystatin will not do much good because the yeast keeps growing back. To treat yeast these foods must be removed from the diet. Removal of these dietary yeast products enables nystatin to kill the yeast without the yeast growing back. Malt contains chains of sugar molecules which most likely inhibit the body's immune system. This inhibition makes it hard for the immune system to fight *Candida*. Malt must be removed to clear *Candida*.

Fortunately, because nystatin is not absorbed, nystatin causes no side effects except for a little nausea. Therefore there is no risk to this therapy.

The diet for *Candida* problems consists of removing fermented foods from the diet. The worst offenders are alcoholic beverages and non-alcoholic beer, vinegar, barley malt, chocolate, pickles, soy sauce and aged cheese. This diet is described in the books *An Extraordinary Power to Heal* and *Feast Without Yeast*.

Every child I have seen who has followed this antiyeast therapy has improved. Children who can speak always speak better and more. Children under two and a half who can talk a little can be brought back to normal or near normal. Behavior and sleep all improve. Children are calmer and easier to teach.

Gluten-Free Casein-Free Diet

Where does the gluten free casein free diet fit in? This diet comes from research on schizophrenia, in which these gluten and casein protein fragments were found in the urine of schizophrenic patients. Similar urine profiles were later found in the urine of autistic children.

The role of opioids in autism is as follows. Milk and dairy contain a protein called casein and wheat contains a protein called gluten. Inside of both casein and gluten are structures which are difficult for the body to digest completely. The structures or peptides remaining after digestion of casein and gluten react at certain sites in the brain called opioid receptors. These sites are so named because these sites are where opiate drugs such as morphine act. The internal chemicals which react at the opioid receptors in the brain are called endorphins. These peptide structures from the diet have several names, one of which is "opioids."

In experimental studies, opiate drugs such as morphine have been found to bind to brain opioid receptors and this binding leads to decreased glucose (sugar) utilization and decreased metabolic rate. In other words structures which bind to opioid receptors in the brain slow the brain down. As already noted, the one finding that stands up in the brains of autistic children is that the brain is slowed down (metabolically less active) as shown by decreased blood flow, especially in speech areas.

Presumably these casein and gluten protein fragments also slow the brain down. This has led to the treatment of excluding casein and gluten from the diet of autistic children. There are many commercial products available to support such treatment.

Using Gluten-Free and Casein-Free Diets

How good is the gluten free casein free diet? The main studies show that children do better in school. In my experience some children improve, some only modestly and some barely at all. Why? The gluten free casein free diet is not an anti-yeast diet. The gluten free casein free diet allows some major yeast offenders such as vinegar, pickles, chocolate, peanut butter and corn. Both peanuts and corn are often contaminated with mold. Chicken are fed much cottonseed and cottonseed is contaminated with mold.

So if a child is taken off gluten and casein but is continued on vinegar and is put on more chicken, peanut butter and corn, what will happen? Whatever benefits there are from removing gluten and casein will be taken away by adding to the diet more mold in the form of chicken, peanut butter and corn. The intestinal yeast will still be there making toxic chemicals. The child will show only minimal improvement and the improvement and behavior will fluctuate, depending on what the child has eaten.

This gluten free casein free diet is often recommended today as the main thing to do for autistic children. However, I recommend the gluten free/casein free diet only after the anti-yeast diet has been started. The gluten free casein free diet allows eating of vinegar, pickles, and other foods containing toxic yeast chemicals which are quite toxic to the brains of autistic children. Except for elimination of malt, there is no overlap between foods eliminated on a gluten free/casein free diet and foods eliminated on Stage 1 of the anti-yeast diet (as described in *An Extraordinary Power to Heal* and *Feast Without Yeast*). Malt (which is actually a specially sprouted barley product) should be eliminated on a gluten free/casein free diet and malt is the number 1 item to eliminate on an anti-yeast diet. However, too many other foods containing toxic chemicals can be left in on a gluten free/casein free diet, to use this diet as the only therapy.

High-Dose Vitamins and Minerals

What about high doses of vitamins and minerals? Vitamin B-6 neutralizes one of the yeast chemicals and this yeast chemical takes the place of magnesium at important sites in the body. The neutralization of this chemical may explain why vitamin B-6 and magnesium are sometimes helpful. However, I think it is much better to clear out the yeast, so that the chemical is no longer made rather than to try to neutralize it. There are many other yeast chemicals which are not affected by vitamin B-6 and magnesium.

Parents who continue the high doses of vitamins and minerals and then try to add nystatin often find that nystatin is not helpful. I suspect that one of the vitamins, perhaps vitamin B-6, binds to nystatin, making it ineffective. I now recommend to parents not to use the high doses of vitamins and minerals while giving nystatin.

Acidophilus

I often get asked about *Acidophilus*. I do not recommend it, because *Acidophilus* helps yeast grow. Initially, *Acidophilus* may seem to help because it clears out another bad microorganism, *Clostridia*, but *acidophilus* does nothing for yeast. *Acidophilus* makes an anti-bacterial chemical. *Acidophilus* should only be used short-term, not long-term.

Specific Carbohydrate Diet

Some people for their autistic children try the specific carbohydrate diet. This diet is used for people with major allergic reactions. This diet is not an anti-yeast diet. This diet consists of simple food molecules which the yeast *Candida* can easily use to grow. For fighting yeast, the specific carbohydrate diet has no place and may make the yeast and the autism worse.

Yeast and the Immune System

Why can the body's immune system not clear *Candida*? The *Candida* has many tricks to evade the body's immune system. The immune system then calls in the reinforcements. These immune cells attack the yeast and generate the signals for inflammation. Inflammation is a defense, like a wall to keep out the *Candida*. The *Candida* is still there, which means the inflammation remains.

In the intestine, this continued inflammation leads to Crohn's disease and ulcerative colitis. Sometimes these immune cells circulate and find yeast cells in other places. There is yeast on the skin. Again the yeast is evasive and the immune cells generate the signals for inflammation. The yeast is not cleared and the inflammation remains. This leads to skin problems from itching and eczema to psoriasis.

The *Candida* has also evolved to look like our own cells. *Candida* has the body's own connective tissue receptor on it, which it uses to anchor itself into our tissues. Sometimes the immune cells, as they attack the yeast, attack anything which looks like the yeast. What else looks like the yeast? Body cells which have the con-

A baker makes gluten-free scones. Products containing low amounts of gluten and yeast have been indicated to help autistic people lessen the effects of the disease. (**AP Images.**)

nective tissue receptor. This attacking of body cells leads to "autoimmune diseases" such as multiple sclerosis and rheumatoid arthritis. In these diseases, the body's immune system appears to be attacking the body's own tissues. The immune cells are attacking the yeast and then attacking anything which looks like the yeast.

More Brain and Body Slow-Down

The yeast chemicals slow the brain down. The gut has its own brain to make sure all the food goes through the intestinal tract at the right rate. What will happen if yeast chemicals put the gut's brain to sleep? The result will be constipation, sometimes very severe. Diarrhea is the body's attempt to clear the yeast. The diarrhea can be present at the same time as the constipation, which is why they can alternate.

What happens if the yeast chemicals slow down the body's nerves and put them to sleep? Then the child can't feel anything or nothing feels right. The hardest parts of the nerves to numb up are the parts which carry pain. This is why light touch, instead of feeling pleasant, now feels painful. If the nerves are numb, sometimes pain feels better than nothing at all. This is why these children bang their heads. Even the pain feels better than numbness.

The lack of proper sensation in the mouth is a reason why these children can become picky eaters. Foods, especially new ones do not feel right to them. The picky eating improves with anti-yeast treatment.

Sleep Problems

Why do autistic children have such trouble sleeping? There are many chemicals which put their brains to sleep. But the brain does not want to go to sleep from these chemicals. How does the brain fight these chemicals? The brain stays awake. When the chemicals are removed, children sleep better. These chemicals also cause headaches and abdominal pain.

Melatonin is a natural hormone made in the brain when it is dark. Melatonin is a signal for people to go to sleep. For unknown reasons, autistic people do not seem to make enough melatonin or perhaps they make enough, but don't respond to it, so they stay awake for long periods of time when other people would be asleep. Giving melatonin at night is helpful in promoting sleep.

Melatonin is available in health food stores and other places. However, be sure to get a brand that contains only melatonin, and is not mixed with vitamins or other substances. Some brands may also contain other allergens, such as wheat or dairy or casein. Look for melatonin mixed in powdered rice. Start with 1/2 capsule (about 1.5 mg.) mixed in a small amount of food, given at the start of bedtime routine, preferably when it is already dark.

Melatonin is not a sleeping pill and does not act like one. You will not see the person drop off suddenly to sleep. Rather, it promotes natural sleep.

Pregnancy

What about pregnancy after having an autistic child? Pregnancy may seem about the scariest thing imaginable after having an autistic child. If we understand that the yeast chemicals cause major disruptions in development, we can reduce the risk of autism by clearing these chemicals. How? A woman who wants to have another child should follow the anti-yeast diet and take nystatin for a few months before becoming pregnant. She should continue this program during pregnancy and while nursing. The child should not be given antibiotics. The child should not be given any foods which help yeast grow.

This program will substantially reduce the risk of a second autistic child.

Using the DIR/Floortime Approach Can Help Treat Autism

Stanley I. Greenspan and Serena Wieder

In the following viewpoint Stanley I. Greenspan and Serena Wieder contend that working to build healthy development rather than just treating symptoms and surface behavior is very effective in the treatment of autism. Treating communication skills, personal interaction skills, and creative and logical thinking skills are the key to helping an autistic individual, they assert. According to the authors the two primary goals of the floortime approach are: to follow the child's lead, using the child's natural interests to build skills, and to bring the child into a world where he or she can participate in activities with others. The authors acknowledge that this approach is very time-consuming and sometimes very frustrating, but in the end, they argue, it is worth the effort.

Greenspan and Wieder are codevelopers of the DIR (Developmental, Individual-Difference, Relationship-Based)/Floortime Approach to treating autism. Wieder is a clinical psychologist and founder of the Floortime Foundation; Greenspan is a clinical professor of psychiatry, behavioral sciences, and pediatrics at George Washington University Medical School.

SOURCE: Stanley I. Greenspan, MD, and Serena Wieder, PhD, *Engaging Autism: Using the Floortime Approach to Help Children Relate, Communicate, and Think.* Danvers, MA: Da Capo Books, 2006.

Floortime is at the heart of both our DIR [Developmental, Individual-Difference, Relationship-Based] model and a comprehensive program for infants and children with a variety of developmental challenges, including ASD [autism spectrum disorders]. . . . A comprehensive program includes working at a child's emotional developmental level, creating learning relationships tailored to his individual processing differences in order to move him up the developmental ladder. This program includes not only Floortime but also different therapies, education programs, counseling support for parents, and intensive home and school programs, as well as other learning opportunities such as play groups, music lessons, gymnastics classes, and so forth. Floortime is at the heart of the home component and can be woven into many other parts of the program.

Floortime is both a specific technique—in which for twenty or more minutes at a time a caregiver gets down on the floor to interact with the child—and a general philosophy that characterizes all daily interactions with the child. Let's look at what Floortime is and what it isn't, and explain why it is the cornerstone of the DIR model and the developmental process.

The Two Goals of Floortime

Floortime has two main goals. Sometimes these two work together easily, and other times they may appear almost in opposition, but both must always be considered. One goal—by far the more widely known and followed—is *to follow the child's lead* or harness the child's natural interests. Why do we follow the child's lead? After all, historically, educators have long held that adults can't just allow children to do what they want to do, because children are creatures of instinct who would never become socialized if we just followed their lead. But in Floortime, we take our cue from the child because a child's interests are the window to her emotional and intellectual life. Through observing the child's interests and natural desires, we get a picture of what she finds enjoyable, what motivates her. If a child is staring at a fan, rubbing a spot on the floor over and over, or always walking on her toes, these might seem actions that we want to discourage. But something about the behavior is meaningful or pleasurable to the child.

Therefore, we always start off by asking the question, "Why is my child doing that?" To say simply that it's because he has this or that disorder doesn't answer the question. The child may have a disorder or a set of problems, but he is not the disorder or set of problems. He is a human being with real feelings, real desires, and real wishes. If children can't express their desires or wishes, we have to deduce what they enjoy from what they are doing. So in Floortime we begin by following the child's lead and joining him in his own world.

The second goal is to bring the child into a shared world. However, we don't want to pull her in kicking and screaming. We want her to *want* to be in the world with us. For a variety of reasons, a child may have elected to be self-absorbed, aimless, or seemingly withdrawn into her own world. Thus the rationale for the first goal: a child feels closer to you if she sees that you can respect and participate in what interests her. . . .

As the child starts giving you some curious or friendly glances, instead of looking annoyed or running away from you, that's the beginning of a shared world. Once the child enjoys participating with us, we can begin helping her master each of the basic abilities of relating, communicating, and thinking. . . . Our ultimate goal for bringing children into a shared world is to help them become empathetic, creative, logical, reflective individuals.

Using the First Floortime Goal

How does "following the child's lead," the first goal of Floortime, help the child master these critical developmental milestones? This gets to the real substance of Floortime. . . .

Floortime Checklist: Questions to Ask

Floortime Checklist: Questions to Ask

Is he:

- engaging with toys (objects) or me?
- reacting or initiating interactions?
- opening and closing a few circles of communication or heading toward a continuous flow?
- labeling or creating his own new ideas in play conversations?
- marching to his own drummer or responding to my ideas as well as his own?

Source: Stanley I. Greenspan and Serena Wieder, *Engaging Autism: Using the Floortime Approach to Help Children Relate, Communicate, and Think*, 2006.

We've worked out a number of strategies that begin with following a child's lead and then continue with enticing the child to really want to learn this new, wonderful ability.

For example, if a child always wants to play with his favorite toy instead of interacting, we may use the strategy . . . of being playfully obstructive: we can gently scoop the toy up, put it on our head and make silly faces, and see if he will reach for it. We could then show him that we are putting it outside the door. When he bangs on the door to get it back, we ask, "Should I help you?" And pretty soon he's taking our hand and putting it on the doorknob. Eventually, he's saying "Open," to get us to open the door to get that favorite toy. So now, through following the child's lead, we have mobilized not just attention, engagement, and purposeful action, but problem-solving and even the beginning use of words. These strategies are useful even for a child who is aimless or avoidant.

Some children have a narrow range of focus and have a hard time integrating attention to people and things at the same time. To help a child with this problem become more interactive with more flexible attention, caregivers should join his play and become one of the characters in the drama. . . . This can encourage a continuous flow of creative dialogue with the child.

Sometimes all that is necessary is to help a child toward his own goals. If a child is moving a truck back and forth and we make our hands into a tunnel, he may look at that, give us a big smile, and move the truck right into our tunnel. Now we have shared attention, engagement, purposeful action, and some problem-solving. Eventually we may introduce the word "truck" and he may repeat it. We can even give him choices: "Do you want to move it into the tunnel or into the house?" He may respond, "Hou—," and point toward the toy house. Then we have thinking occurring along with the use of words.

Following the Lead

In Floortime, we follow the child's lead to enter his emotional world, then create a series of opportunities and challenges to help him move up to higher levels of relating, communicating, and thinking. While challenging children to master new milestones, we are always trying to strengthen and broaden their current abilities. If they can be a little purposeful, we want them to be more purposeful. If they can open and close three or four circles of communication, we want to increase that to eight, and then to ten, and on until we get to more than fifty. If they have a few words, we want to stretch these into conversations.

In doing all this, of course, we have to tailor our strategies to the child's individual processing differences. . . . We also need to pay attention to ourselves as caregivers. What are our natural strengths and weaknesses? What do we do easily? A high-energy person is great for kids who underreact and need a lot of energizing and wooing, but that person may have a harder time soothing the child. A calm person may be a great soother for hypersensitive children, but have a hard time energizing up for an underreactive child. If a child avoids us, do we take it as a personal rejection and either shut down and stop trying or get too intrusive and try to force her to pay attention to us? Asking those difficult questions, we can then fine-tune our strategies to meet the child's special sensitivities and needs.

Floortime Learning

Floortime is not about doing a right or wrong thing; it's a process in which you and your child are always learning. Following the child's lead doesn't mean commenting about or just imitating what he is doing; it means getting in there and interacting with him on the basic level of his interest. Because you have to give the child a reason to want to play with you, it's important to start out by observing for a few moments so you can discover what his true interests are. Those interests may go beyond his specific behavior. For example, he may be lining up toys, but his broader interest might be to create order or fixed patterns or a certain design. If he is setting his toys in a straight line, you might offer another toy for his line, or playfully challenge him by putting a toy at a right angle to his line with a big smile. In either case, you might get a nice interaction. Once he sees that you are not going to stop him or pull him away, he might pause and look, after he puts another toy in the line, to see if you'll put the next toy in the lineup. So think of yourself primarily as a player.

Once a child can stop worrying that you are going to interfere with what she wants to do, she will let you join in and play because playing together is actually more fun. Help the child do what she wants to do. Break a motor problem down into little pieces, for example, if the child wants to open a container, find a toy, or reach a shelf. Depending on the child, you may use toys in the interaction, or you may just use yourself and some very simple objects. If your child loves to run and climb, you can make that interactive by being a human obstacle course—she will figure out what you are doing and begin to work around it. You're looking for the moment when she realizes, "Oh, this is a game!"

After the Session Ends

After a Floortime session is over, step back and analyze what happened. Try to think about what it is that gets in the way of the flow of interactions. If both parents are available each can take turns coaching the other. Are you using visual cues and strategies? Is your tone of voice lively and energizing or soothing and quiet? Remember, your voice is probably the most powerful tool you have to cue your child. Whether or not the child understands the words, the message comes from the tone, rhythm, loudness, and pacing of your voice. Find out how it is you stay connected to your child.

> **FAST FACT**
>
> A case study of two hundred children with autistic spectrum disorder who received DIR/Floortime therapy showed that 58 percent had "good to outstanding" outcomes.

One of the most important things is to meet the child at his current developmental level. Parents often are disappointed that their child isn't playing the way they think he should be. If that enters your mind, it's an indication that you are not following the child's lead enough. To help the child be more purposeful, we want to treat what he is doing as purposeful. Start out by helping him to do what he wants to do, then try to expand on that with him. If he is playing with a car and suddenly starts to move on, you might see if he wants to have some other cars, and before you know it, you'll be building a garage together. Worry not so much about what you do next as about staying within what your child already started; this is critical if you are going to bring more depth and elaboration to that activity or interest.

Using Objects and Symbols in Floortime

Fostering engagement and a continuous flow of interaction is always a primary goal of Floortime. So is helping the child to interact with objects and people together and to create symbols or ideas.

Children often love specific objects or toys, such as a dinosaur they use for everything. Accept your child's objects. Whether it's Barney or a Sesame Street character or a teddy bear, your child's plaything will give you some indication of her emotional life and what she finds meaningful. When the child is ready to use toys in Floortime, you can focus on generating the interactive flow around that particular toy. It could be as simple as making a slide. If you put a figure on top of a slide, you can inevitably get a child to push the figure down the slide. Think about the favorite toy as a friend that you can use to play with together.

Giving the Toy Meaning

Once the child is playing with a toy, see if you can help the child to give it symbolic meaning. For example, as your child is eating, talk for a favorite doll and ask for food: "Feed me, please!" One day your child may delight you by putting food near the doll's mouth. With this kind of prompting, the child might begin to elaborate his play around familiar experiences, incorporating dollhouses, doctor kits, tool kits, and so forth. But be sure that the child chooses it, so that it is meaningful to him. Then you can introduce something that responds to what your child did. The magic words in elaboration are, "What else? What else can we do?" The real goal is to keep that interaction going.

Take a good look at whether you are providing all the support the child needs in terms of his specific processing abilities, regulatory system, and interest and initiative and also in the way you respond yourself. If your child is distracted, you want to be sure you're not the one

Paul DeSavino, diagnosed with autism as a child, practices piano at a group home. Socialization skills can help autistic people overcome their illness. (**AP Images.**)

distracting him. Try to see what makes him get stuck. Trust that this is a process—there is no right or wrong answer—and if something doesn't work, just follow the child's next step, and you'll have another chance to get a more elaborate game going.

Don't worry about the content; we can't move the content ahead of the process. We won't get elaborate symbolic stories and much pretend play in any form unless we get a nice lively interaction going first. Rather than pushing the child up the developmental ladder, focus on deepening the level where the child is already, because that is where he'll have the most ability to become fully engaged. There is no rush in Floortime. If you're not sure what to do, step back and see what your child is up to, reconnect, and then expand on that connection. We mobilize children's development by being players with them.

When Floortime Seems Too Difficult

The main reason parents avoid doing Floortime or avoid emotional interactions with their children is that, deep down (often not consciously), they fear they can't do it. Often parents tell us, once we've stripped away some of the surface defenses, "No one ever played with me this way, and I don't think I can do it. I think the best I could do is just change my child's behavior." Other parents get stuck during Floortime; they feel they have used up their bag of tricks and that nothing they do seems to work.

My advice in these situations is always the same: Don't pressure yourself to do so much. Whenever you feel stuck, take a step back, relax, and observe what the child is doing. The child may not seem to be doing much; she may just be playing with her own fingers. But that is something. A child is always doing something. Ask yourself how you can build on it. Joining one of your fingers with hers, or any other strategy that helps your child relate to you, could work. For children who are extremely challenging, sometimes the best way to start a relationship is through simple, sensory-based play, such as lying on the floor together, rolling over each other, and making funny noises, or simple holding and rhythmic rocking. There's no substitute for warm, joyful relatedness.

What this all boils down to is finding something you and your child can enjoy together. Often that requires exploring which rhythmic movement, touch, or sound game is mutually enjoyable. While you may not love crawling on the floor with your child, you'll enjoy his pleasure in this shared activity. Once you get that joyful relating going, don't be afraid to incorporate things you know he loves, such as a favorite toy, food treat, or game.

You can provide several options and then the child can choose among them.

Ultimately . . . you want to challenge the child to take the initiative. For example, if the child enjoys riding around on your shoulders, after doing this for a bit, you might stand still and challenge her to gesture, make a sound, or somehow indicate where she wants you to go before you'll go anywhere. When giving the child a back rub, let her show you where to rub—arms, back, or tummy.

Whenever play is repetitive, vary what you do. This challenges the child to vary what he does, even if it's within the same basic action or the same basic game. Once the interaction is moving forward, and there is attention, engagement, and purposeful communication with gestures and maybe words, then the goal—and this can be the hardest thing to achieve for children with ASD—is to get the child interacting and communicating for ten to fifteen minutes at a time. We see many children with ASD who are already reading, doing math, and using long whole sentences but who can't have a long shared conversation.

To summarize, Floortime involves following the child's lead and pulling him into your world, then going beyond that by challenging him to master each of the developmental levels. It requires paying attention to the child's individual processing differences and nervous system, to family patterns, and to your own personality (to learn how you need to stretch to work with the child).

Using ABA Therapy Can Help Treat Autism

S. Jhoanna Robledo and Dawn Ham-Kucharski

In the following selection the authors state that Applied Behavior Analysis (ABA) is the most common intervention therapy used with autistic children. ABA improves communication, social skills, and play skills. It is also used to help foster independence. Working with the parents, an ABA therapist designs an individualized approach to helping the autistic child improve skills and behavior. One of the biggest advantages to ABA therapy, say the authors, is that its methods have been used for many years and have proven results. The most common drawback to this approach is that, like any therapy, it does not work for every autistic child.

Robledo is a writer and a graduate of the Columbia School of Journalism. Ham-Kucharski is a member of the board of directors of the Michigan Autism Partnership and the parent of an autistic child.

SOURCE: S. Jhoanna Robledo and Dawn Ham-Kucharski, *The Autism Book*. New York: The Penguin Group, 2005. Copyright © 2005 by S. Jhoanna Robledo and Dawn Ham-Kucharski. All rights reserved. Used by permission of Avery Publishing, an imprint of Penguin Group (USA) Inc.

Applied Behavioral Analysis (ABA) is by far the most common education and intervention plan followed by parents of autistic children. A few variations exist, but the program that's proven popular, known as the UCLA Model of Applied Behavior Analysis, is the brainchild of Dr. O. Ivar Lovaas, the executive director of the Lovaas Institute for Early Intervention in Los Angeles, California. ABA is an approach rooted in the fundamentals of behavior modification, which many psychologists employ in treating all sorts of physical, mental, and emotional disorders.

ABA plays a large role in many educational programs designed especially for autistic children. It's meant to improve communication skills, foster social interaction, encourage play, and help autistic kids become more independent. Vanessa Jenses, executive director of the Cleveland Clinic's Center for Autism, which uses ABA as the foundation for its interventions and strategies, says it does so by using a "systematic application of behavioral treatment" to change the behavior of children with autism and PDD [pervasive developmental disorders].

ABA practitioners approach their work by understanding that autism is a developmental disorder, one that's biological and neurological in nature and that can be tracked by studying brain functioning and behavior. Autistic children, unlike other kids, aren't "wired" to interpret the world and the people in it as easily or as clearly as the rest of us. A light touch may feel like a shove; basic eye contact may come across as debilitatingly intrusive; a whisper can seem as loud as a sonic boom. Add to these experiences the autistic child's inability to let grown-ups know exactly how they're feeling and filtering all this stimuli, and you have a child who may seem, to those who are

> **FAST FACT**
>
> Almost half the children who received forty hours per week of ABA therapy were eventually able to complete normal first-grade classes, while none of the children who received ten hours per week were able to do so.

uneducated about autism or are unaware the child is autistic, out of control, over-reactive, or cold and distant.

The responses of autistic children are all they know; but these kids can be taught new ways of managing and responding to the world. Through educational methods such as discrete trials, prompting, and reinforcement, kids who follow the ABA program set target goals of behavior and reach them by approaching each new situation with a toolbox of skills they've acquired through repeated practice and drills. ABA professionals work on helping kids to master socially acceptable behaviors and to give up inappropriate ones. Success in one area (eye contact, for example) may lead to attempting even bigger goals (saying "hello" during personal introductions, for one).

What first takes place if you choose to venture down the ABA path is a diagnostic assessment, which examines your child's behavioral issues, how long your child has exhibited them, the reasons to which you attribute these behaviors, and what happens when your child acts in a particular manner.

After this evaluation, your child's ABA therapist, with your input, devises an individualized plan of action and implements it in one-on-one sessions. During these meetings, an effective ABA therapist studies closely the "cause-and-effect" relationships between a situation and your child's reaction. She examines her method as she teaches your child a skill as well as the characteristics of the environment that may have an effect on your child's response, and then tries to accurately measure the effects.

At these sessions, you, as parents, are expected to watch and learn so you can then use the same strategies to help your child on your own; it's important that you're able to implement the same strategies at home. After all, consistency is vital, since varying from the norm may make it difficult for the ABA therapist and you to evaluate what truly works and what doesn't. In between ap-

How ABA Therapy Works

This diagram demonstrates how Applied Behavior Analysis (ABA) works, using the combined resources of family members, occupational therapists (OT), speech-language pathologist (SLP), teachers, and the ABA team.

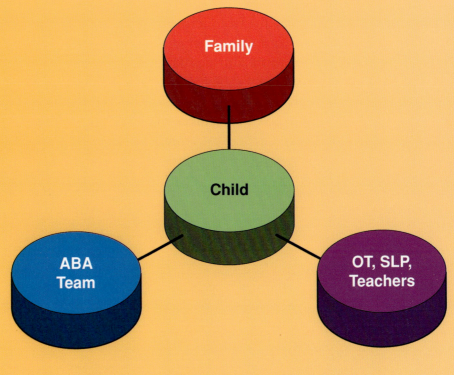

Source: Patricia Rich, ABA Treatment Center, 2007. www.trishrichbcba.com.

pointments, you may be asked to keep a diary of your child's problematic behaviors (such as banging his head against a wall or scratching your face), noting what may have triggered them, how you responded, and how your child met that response. Parents of children with severe autism often elect to augment the sessions with a formalized home-based program in which they're taught techniques and activities in which they can engage their kids at home. They check in periodically with an ABA center's staff members for feedback and advice, and home visits are scheduled.

Here's a simplified example of what may take place at an ABA one-on-one session: Let's say the ABA therapist is working with a child on completing a simple puzzle. They sit at a table across from each other at eye level. Whereas your child normally throws pieces of a puzzle across the room, during the session they practice putting the pieces of a puzzle together. When the child manages to complete the puzzle on his own, for example, the therapist may give him a piece of fruit, a cookie, a favorite

Three autistic children learn how to surf at Alii Beach Park in Haleiwa, Hawaii. Skills such as balance and socialization may help patients combat autism. **(AP Images.)**

toy, or even a tickle. The therapist then records the child's response. When improvements in behavior appear to be on their way to becoming permanent, the tangible rewards are phased out, replaced by a child's developing ability to discern the pleasing results that their appropriate behavior engenders in others.

Some say ABA is based in part on research by theorist/scientist B.F. Skinner, who found that behavior could be molded through a process called "operant conditioning." In some of his experiments, animals were taught behaviors (e.g., getting a rat to use an automatic food dispenser) that, if mastered, resulted in them getting a reward. While ABA experts don't claim that kids should be trained the same way animals are, children—autistic or not—do learn through repetition, and this is the cornerstone of ABA's philosophy. According to Leslie Sinclair, program director at the Cleveland Clinic's Center for Autism, toddlers do well with intensive, one-on-one therapy. The repetitive nature of ABA drives home its lessons, and as they learn how to behave they can master new skills.

Autistic kids may not easily grasp the concept of learning, but they discover, through the help of their ABA therapist, how to better understand the learning process. In essence, writes Richard Saffran, father of an autistic child and an expert in ABA, they "learn to learn." When one-on-one sessions are over, the regimen is continued at home, tackling more complex skills as the child grows older. Ideally, the treatment plan continues in a classroom that uses ABA as the foundation for the school's educational philosophies.

ABA's biggest asset may be its longevity. Its stature as the most established of treatment strategies for autistic children gives it much-deserved credibility, as do the reams of data and studies that have shown its success in helping kids function happily and well in society. In 1987, Lovaas published groundbreaking research that showed that the drills that make up a large portion of the

ABA method were successful in helping autistic children, some of whom exhibited such great gains that they no longer appeared to be on the spectrum. Autism expert Richard L. Simpson, writing in the summer 2001 issue of the journal *Focus on Autism and Other Developmental Disabilities*, observed that there is "overwhelming evidence that methods based on the behaviorally based principles of ABA form the foundation of many effective individualized programs and generally bode well for achievement of desired outcomes among individuals with autism spectrum disorders." In plain English, ABA works for lots of autistic kids. And ABA proponents have tons of research to prove it.

Another reason autistic children who follow ABA are successful is the program's emphasis on one-on-one instruction, at least in the initial stages. With such close study, an ABA therapist can keep a watchful eye on what's working and what's not, and tailor the sessions accordingly. Although it's not required of a successful regimen, one-on-one sessions ensure your child gets a great deal of individualized attention.

Even though children in ABA environments participate in drills, and they're expected to learn a set of skills—a "curriculum" of sorts—these sessions cannot, by any means, be described as cookie-cutter. Instead, you and your therapist work together to come up with the best strategy, using the science of ABA, for your child.

Does ABA Have Any Shortcomings?

Like any other approach, ABA doesn't work for every child. One of the biggest disadvantages of committing to a true ABA treatment plan (one that includes extensive one-on-one sessions and evaluations, training and materials) is how much you could end up paying for it. Plainly put, ABA can be prohibitively expensive. It can cost as much as, if not more than, tuition at a top-notch private elementary school, running in the tens of thousands of dollars each year. Fees covering ten months of training at the Princeton Child Development Institute in New Jersey, a nationally renowned research, treatment, and ABA-based educational center for autistic children, total more than $45,000 wrote Iver Peterson in a May 2000 front-page story in the *New York Times*. A portion of the expenses may be covered by insurance, but most parents eke out a way to pay out of pocket. Learning ABA methods and then opting for a home-based approach is one way to cut the costs, but studies show that children are likelier to thrive in an ABA classroom or one-on-one environment.

Some parents gripe that ABA is far too rigid and that "training" children feels "unnatural" or "forced." They complain that the technique of repetition teaches autistic kids only to respond to specific cues, and doesn't help them change their approach to events in everyday life. They use the old argument that it's like giving a man a fish so he can eat for one day instead of teaching him how to fish so he'll learn how to eat for the rest of his life.

But as with the other interventions, it matters where you go for help and whom you consult. An institution may claim to subscribe to the ABA method, but may not train its teachers adequately in it so they can actually make a difference in the lives of their young clients.

In his *Times* article, Peterson described ABA as "very expensive . . . coaching." Kathy Mannion, executive director for the Association for Science in Autism Treatment immediately objected to that notion, expressing her dissent in a letter to the *Times* editor in which she asserted that ABA is "the only treatment intervention for autism that has withstood scientific scrutiny for more than thirty years." In many cases, parents sign up for the classes, and as they master the techniques themselves, discontinue training (thereby saving money) and apply what they learn at home until it's almost second nature.

SONGS

of the

GORILLA

NATION

{ MY JOURNEY THROUGH AUTISM

Visual Autism: An Autistic's Experience

Temple Grandin

Temple Grandin has a PhD in animal science and has designed numerous livestock handling facilities in the United States. She is also an associate professor of animal science at Colorado State University.

In the following selection Grandin talks about an aspect of her life with autism. She discusses how she sees things very differently from other people. Instead of seeing things in terms of words, she sees things in terms of pictures; everything she reads or hears is translated into pictures in her brain. To recall something that was said she must recall the picture that the words formed in her mind. According to Grandin this has given her a unique perspective in which to study animal behavior and design livestock equipment. She has been able to use her autism to great advantage.

Photo on facing page. Books such as this one help outsiders understand autism. (AP Images.)

I think in pictures. Words are like a second language to me. I translate both spoken and written words into full-color movies, complete with sound, which run like a VCR tape in my head. When somebody speaks to me, his words are instantly translated into pictures. Language-based thinkers often find this phenomenon difficult to understand, but in my job as an equipment designer for the livestock industry, visual thinking is a tremendous advantage.

Visual thinking has enabled me to build entire systems in my imagination. During my career I have designed all kinds of equipment, ranging from corrals for handling cattle on ranches to systems for handling cattle and hogs during veterinary procedures and slaughter. I have worked for many major livestock companies. In fact, one third of the cattle and hogs in the United States are handled in equipment I have designed. Some of the people I've worked for don't even know that their systems were designed by someone with autism. I value my ability to think visually, and I would never want to lose it.

One of the most profound mysteries of autism has been the remarkable ability of most autistic people to excel at visual spatial skills while performing so poorly at verbal skills. When I was a child and a teenager, I thought everybody thought in pictures. I had no idea that my thought processes were different. In fact, I did not realize the full extent of the differences until very recently. At meetings and at work I started asking other people detailed questions about how they accessed information from their memories. From their answers I learned that my visualization skills far exceeded those of most other people.

I credit my visualization abilities with helping me understand the animals I work with. Early in my career I used a camera to help give me the animals' perspective as they walked through a chute for their veterinary treatment. I would kneel down and take pictures through the chute from the cow's eye level. Using the photos, I was able to figure out which things scared the cattle, such as shadows and bright spots of sunlight. Back then I used black-and-white film, because twenty years ago scientists believed that cattle lacked color vision. Today, research has shown that cattle can see colors, but the photos provided the unique advantage of seeing the world through a cow's viewpoint. They helped me figure out why the animals refused to go in one chute but willingly walked through another.

Every design problem I've ever solved started with my ability to visualize and see the world in pictures. I started designing things as a child, when I was always

Temple Grandin, an animal scientist at Colorado State University, sits in a corral at CSU in Fort Collins, Colorado. (AP Images.)

experimenting with new kinds of kites and model airplanes. In elementary school I made a helicopter out of a broken balsa-wood airplane. When I wound up the propeller, the helicopter flew straight up about a hundred feet. I also made bird-shaped paper kites, which I flew behind my bike. The kites were cut out from a single sheet of heavy drawing paper and flown with thread. I experimented with different ways of bending the wings to increase flying performance. Bending the tips of the wings up made the kite fly higher. Thirty years later, this same design started appearing on commercial aircraft.

Now, in my work, before I attempt any construction, I test-run the equipment in my imagination. I visualize my designs being used in every possible situation, with different sizes and breeds of cattle and in different weather conditions. Doing this enables me to correct mistakes prior to construction. Today, everyone is excited about the new virtual reality computer systems in which the user wears special goggles and is fully immersed in video game action. To me, these systems are like crude cartoons. My imagination works like the computer graphics programs that created the lifelike dinosaurs in *Jurassic Park*. When I do an equipment simulation in my imagination or work on an engineering problem, it is like seeing it on a videotape in my mind. I can view it from any angle, placing myself above or below the equipment and rotating it at the same time. I don't need a fancy graphics program that can produce three-dimensional design simulations. I can do it better and faster in my head.

I create new images all the time by taking many little parts of images I have in the video library in my imagination and piecing them together. I have video memories of every item I've ever worked with—steel gates, fences, latches, concrete walls, and so forth. To create new designs, I retrieve bits and pieces from my memory and combine them into a new whole. My design ability keeps improving as I add more visual images to my library. I add video-like images from either actual experiences or translations of written information into pictures. I can visualize the operation of such things as squeeze chutes, truck loading ramps, and all different types of livestock equipment. The more I actually work with cattle and operate equipment, the stronger my visual memories become. . . .

Being autistic, I don't naturally assimilate information that most people take for granted. Instead, I store information in my head as if it were on a CD-ROM disc. When I recall something I have learned, I replay the video in my imagination. The videos in my memory are always specific; for example, I remember handling cattle at the veterinary chute at Producer's Feedlot or McElhaney Cattle Company. I remember exactly how the animals behaved in that specific situation and how the chutes and other equipment were built. The exact construction of steel fenceposts and pipe rails in each case is also part of my visual memory. I can run these images over and over and study them to solve design problems.

If I let my mind wander, the video jumps in a kind of free association from fence construction to a particular welding shop where I've seen posts being cut and Old John, the welder, making gates. If I continue thinking about Old John welding a gate, the video image changes to a series of short scenes of building gates on several projects I've worked on. Each video memory triggers another in this associative fashion, and my daydreams may wander far from the design problem. The next image may be of having a good time listening to John and the construction crew tell war stories, such as the time the backhoe dug into a nest of rattlesnakes and the machine was abandoned for two weeks because everybody was afraid to go near it.

This process of association is a good example of how my mind can wander off the subject. People with more severe autism have difficulty stopping endless associations. I am able to stop them and get my mind back on track. When I find my mind wandering too far away from a design problem I am trying to solve, I just tell myself to get back to the problem. . . .

Processing Nonvisual Information

Autistics have problems learning things that cannot be thought about in pictures. The easiest words for an autistic child to learn are nouns, because they directly relate to pictures. Highly verbal autistic children like I was can sometimes learn how to read with phonics. Written words were too abstract for me to remember, but I could laboriously remember the approximately fifty phonetic sounds and a few rules. Lower-functioning children often learn better by association, with the aid of word labels attached to objects in their environment. Some very impaired autistic children learn more easily if words are spelled out with plastic letters they can feel.

Spatial words such as "over" and "under" had no meaning for me until I had a visual image to fix them in my memory. Even now, when I hear the word "under" by itself, I automatically picture myself getting under the cafeteria tables at school during an air-raid drill, a common occurrence on the East Coast during the early fifties. The first memory that any single word triggers is almost always a childhood memory. I can remember the teacher telling us to be quiet and walking single-file into the cafeteria, where six or eight children huddled under each table. If I continue on the same train of thought, more and more associative memories of elementary school emerge. I can remember the teacher scolding me after I hit Alfred for putting dirt on my shoe.

All of these memories play like videotapes in the VCR in my imagination. If I allow my mind to keep associating, it will wander a million miles away from the word "under," to submarines under the Antarctic and the Beatles song "Yellow Submarine." If I let my mind pause on the picture of the yellow submarine, I then hear the song.

As I start humming the song and get to the part about people coming on board, my association switches to the gangway of a ship I saw in Australia.

I also visualize verbs. The word jumping triggers a memory of jumping hurdles at the mock Olympics held at my elementary school. Adverbs often trigger inappropriate images—"quickly" reminds me of Nestle's Quik—unless they are paired with a verb, which modifies my visual image. For example, "he ran quickly" triggers an animated image of Dick from the first-grade reading book running fast, and "he walked slowly" slows the image down. As a child, I left out words such as "is," "the," and "it," because they had no meaning by themselves. Similarly, words like "of" and "an" made no sense. Eventually I learned how to use them properly, because my parents always spoke correct English and I mimicked their speech patterns. To this day certain verb conjugations, such as "to be," are absolutely meaningless to me.

When I read, I translate written words into color movies or I simply store a photo of the written page to be read later. When I retrieve the material, I see a photocopy of the page in my imagination. I can then read it like a TelePrompTer. It is likely that Raymond, the autistic savant depicted in the movie *Rain Man*, used a similar strategy to memorize telephone books, maps, and other information. He simply photocopied each page of the phone book into his memory. When he wanted to find a certain number, he just scanned pages of the phone book that were in his mind. To pull information out of my memory, I have to replay the video. Pulling facts up quickly is sometimes difficult, because I have to play bits of different videos until I find the right tape. This takes time.

When I am unable to convert text to pictures, it is usually because the text has no concrete meaning. Some

> ## FAST FACT
>
> Because autistic people tend to think in visual terms, many display impressive abilities with jigsaw puzzles and orienting themselves in an unfamiliar city.

philosophy books and articles about the cattle futures market are simply incomprehensible. It is much easier for me to understand written text that describes something that can be easily translated into pictures. The following sentence from a story in the February 21, 1994, issue of *Time* magazine, describing the Winter Olympics figure-skating championships, is a good example: "All the elements are in place—the spotlights, the swelling waltzes and jazz tunes, the sequined sprites taking to the air." In my imagination I see the skating rink and skaters. However, if I ponder too long on the word "elements," I will make the inappropriate association of a periodic table on the wall of my high school chemistry classroom. Pausing on the word "sprite" triggers an image of a Sprite can in my refrigerator instead of a pretty young skater.

Teachers who work with autistic children need to understand associative thought patterns. An autistic child will often use a word in an appropriate manner. Sometimes these uses have a logical associative meaning and other times they don't. For example, an autistic child might say the word "dog" when he wants to go outside. The word "dog" is associated with going outside. In my own case, I can remember both logical and illogical use of inappropriate words. When I was six, I learned to say "prosecution." I had absolutely no idea what it meant, but it sounded nice when I said it, so I used it as an exclamation every time my kite hit the ground. I must have baffled more than a few people who heard me exclaim "Prosecution!" to my downward-spiraling kite.

Discussions with other autistic people reveal similar visual styles of thinking about tasks that most people do sequentially. An autistic man who composes music told me that he makes "sound pictures" using small pieces of other music to create new compositions. A computer programmer with autism told me that he sees the general pattern of the program tree. After he visualizes the skeleton for the program, he simply writes the code for each branch. I use similar methods when I review scientific literature and troubleshoot at meat plants. I take specific findings or observations and combine them to find new basic principles and general concepts.

My thinking pattern always starts with specifics and works toward generalization in an associational and nonsequential way. As if I were attempting to figure out what the picture on a jigsaw puzzle is when only one third of the puzzle is completed, I am able to fill in the missing pieces by scanning my video library. Chinese mathematicians who can make large calculations in their heads work the same way. At first they need an abacus, the Chinese calculator, which consists of rows of beads on wires in a frame. They make calculations by moving the rows of beads. When a mathematician becomes really skilled, he simply visualizes the abacus in his imagination and no longer needs a real one. The beads move on a visualized video abacus in his brain.

Our Son's Special Relationship with Animals

Susan Kirkman and John Kirkman

Susan and John Kirkman are the parents of an autistic young adult living in England. As described in the following article, the Kirkmans' son has a love-hate relationship with animals and other elements of the natural world. The authors explain that their son Tom has always been afraid of dogs, and that the appearance of a dog can send Tom into a panic. Small animals like rabbits and hamsters and large farm animals like cows and horses, however, are not a problem with Tom. The Kirklands explain that Tom has never gotten over his fear of some animals. They plan to continue therapy to help their son deal with his fears.

We have a 19-year-old son, Thomas, who has severe autism and a complex communication disorder. Tom has a love-hate relationship with the natural world which we would like to share with you.

SOURCE: Susan and John Kirkman, "Autism and the Animal World," *The National Autistic Society*, 2007. Reproduced by permission of the publisher and the author.

Tom has always found dogs terrifying, ever since he was a toddler. We have no clear idea why. Perhaps he finds them unpredictable and uncontrollable in their darting bounciness. We know he is typical of people with autism in being hypersensitive to sound. Dogs bark and whine without warning and, as far as Tom knows, cannot be stopped. As he has never been attacked by a dog, his fear doesn't seem to relate to any particular event.

When we walk round town, we have to be constantly aware of where dogs are, were or might be. Tom never forgets a dog location. The phenomenal autistic memory and good spatial sense combine to give an excellent, mental 'dog map'. On our way to local pubs, we always have to zigzag across the road to avoid known dog spots. "Oh, it's a dog!" is the alarm call for action, to hold Tom, to get between him and the dog. Tom is never allowed to walk next to the kerb, because he will unthinkingly (lack of common sense!) run into the road, however busy it might be. Once, he took refuge on the white line down the centre of a busy road in Sheffield!

Behind our house lies Poynton Woods, excellent for birds, jogging, morning and evening strolls, and, of course, dog-walkers. Tom loves these woods but the appearance of a dog sends him into a frenzy.

Dog owners, of course, are at great pains to soothe, to explain that the dogs are peaceful and harmless (how many times have we heard that?); they totally fail to realise the depth of Tom's fear and its fundamental irrationality. We and his school have both tried the same tactic: hold Tom and tell him to stand still and stay calm. We rehearse this at home and in the classroom, so it becomes a mantra. At times, Tom manages it in practice but he is still more likely to charge off yelling, "Stand still, stay calm!" An important point for any concerned parent is the need to persist, practise, persevere. Don't give up. It may take you years, but you might see an improvement. For example, at Alderwasley School, Tom took part in an animal management course. One afternoon they were visited by the police dog-handling unit. Tom did not run away and went so far as to approach and amazingly enough, to us, to pat one of the dogs.

In the summer of 1994, Tom went with us to the Norfolk Wildlife Centre. Tom, still in a pushchair, was an unwilling visitor, refusing to look at anything until we reached the Arctic fox pound, sunken, with a surrounding wall. Tom surprised the three of us by jumping from his pushchair, climbing the wall and trying to leap in to play with the startled foxes.

Tom grew up with a cat, Lucy, the house cat, gentle, arthritic, scared of mice, who died when Tom was seven; she did not frighten him. He did not fuss with her, but neither did he avoid her. Then, inexplicably, when Tom was about 14, a fear of cats set in and has become as strong now as the canine phobia. Since cats are less housebound and more independently mobile than dogs, he has no feline mental map. The main cat problem now is Louise, a beautiful black and white creature who lives between us and Tom's favourite pub. Unfortunately, Louise is extremely friendly, spends hours surveying local events from her front garden or car roof, and always runs to greet passers-by.

Tension builds up as we approach, Tom has to be held, he runs, puts his fingers in his ears; we position ourselves between Tom and the fearsome predator, we get past.

Tom adores pre-school videos starring cats and dogs, such as Garfield and Bagpuss. We assume that this is because, on video, they are completely under control and make no darts in his direction. They are totally separate from live cats and dogs, and because there is so little connection between boxes, Tom remains terrified of softie Louise, whom he cannot control. Once again, there is no possibility of talking with him about it. As with all his videos, particular snatches come into and out of favour, and are played over and over again before being discarded. We are often called in to share these moments, when Tom laughs until he cries.

Smaller creatures cause no problem. Hamsters, guinea pigs and rabbits have lived and died around the house without upsetting Tom. Nor are hefty and imposing animals a source of worry. He will walk merrily through fields of sheep, horses and cattle. Here, he has to protect his mother and sister!

Zoos now are a joy rather than an issue, especially since our visits have included Twycross in Leicestershire and the West Midlands Safari Park. We took him to the safari park when he was fourteen and fifteen. Yes, there was some tension, and for part of the time he hid in the back foot-section of the car protected by his sister, but he gazed appreciatively at rhinos, tigers, camels and deer. Even the llama pushing its head through the window was manageable.

What he hated were the monkeys swarming over the car, looking through windows front and back, pulling off badges and wiper blades. Tom was terrified; for him, it was like being in a glass cage of cats and dogs. Everything was wrong: sudden movements, damage, no chance of controlling the animals or of driving away, because other families loved the monkeys and were driving along in front of us at a snail's pace.

On the other hand, at the end of the route through were the giraffes. They strode elegantly between and around the cars, leaning down to look through the sunroof. Tom's head went up and up; he gazed, rapt. He has loved giraffes ever since and has fluffy versions of them in his room, some babies, some three feet tall. They are grouped so that they can enjoy watching videos with him.

On his first visit to the West Midlands Safari Park, we joined the crowds in the gift shop. Tom's mum, Sue, was always keen to teach Tom moderation, and to do as he was told. The instruction 'One toy, Tom, one' was frequently repeated. Tom listened with no great grace. One toy selected; a second; then a third was grabbed and Tom did his cheetah impersonation out of the shop, bypassing the till and heading out of the exit door. Explanations were hurriedly made by long-suffering parents once we returned him from his great escape.

Before he was ten, insects caused no great problem. We find this surprising, because we believe that Tom dislikes cats, dogs and even babies because they are unpredictable and uncontrollable; clearly the characteristics of insects. As an infant, bee stings seemed not to upset him unduly. Perhaps this was to be expected, because people with autism appear to feel pain differently, not recognising what usually counts as severe pain but being agitated by what most neurotypical people would not find stressful. At 19, Tom still hates being stroked (most of the time) and what is intended as a soothing movement actually jangles his nerves.

The cottage in Brittany that we holidayed in for three years received plenty of visiting flies. We didn't invite them, but the fly screen was often left open. Tom showed no fear of the flies, but wanted the air to be fly-free, so used a small plastic swat to hunt them down. This took patience and perseverance, and of course, people with autism display this aplenty if it's towards a goal they value, so there was no let-up until each intruder was dispatched. It also took a lot of skill and dexterity, because flies have an amazing ability to see nearby movements and have a superbly short reaction time. Nevertheless, Tom could rise to any fly gauntlet thrown down, and happily spent hours a day keeping the cottage air insect free.

Things are very different now. Tom's vocabulary includes wasp, beetle, spider, bee, fly and moth, and he hates them all. He cannot share a room with one. Of an evening, from his room we might hear "Do something!" or "Help

Small animals can be comforting to autistic children, while larger ones can cause intense panic. **(AP Images.)**

me!" and know we have to remove the offender, however cunningly or awkwardly it has hidden itself. We know of no event that changed Tom's perception so drastically.

Birds interest Tom. He will look at large and obvious birds and can recognise and mimic the calls or songs of heron, crow, jay, magpie, tawny owl and robin. We live in an area with a good heron population, and Tom acts out well how they hunt their food. Seeing one flying overhead, he volunteered, "Heron, long beak." One often sits on top of a nearby conifer, looking foolish and out of place; Tom likes to watch it.

For no reason we know of, smaller birds are of less interest and are not distinguished one from another at home, although at school he worked on a garden bird project and fed them from a table the students made.

In common with many people with autism, we think that Tom sees things as being in boxes, and separate ones at that. A nesting hierarchy of categories, and Venn diagrams, are not how Tom's mind operates. I write that he sees things in boxes but we cannot be sure, for we do not know how Tom sees or links visual objects with words in his brain. However, we do know that for years, Tom would become cross if we said that crows or robins are birds. A typical reply would be, "Don't be silly, father, that's not a bird it's a crow." Or sometimes he would be more direct: "Rubbish, father!"

To Tom, there were hundreds of types of creatures, all birds, but not integrated into an overall bird category. Constant use of terms such as crow-bird, heron-bird, or saying 'it's a magpie; thats a bird' seem to be helping to form the idea of categories, though we cannot tell whether it is implicit or explicit.

Despite constant reassurance and efforts, we have made little headway on the cat and dog front. As always with youngsters with autism, we continue to chip away. Our next steps are to take up the offer of a friend who has a laid back and amenable dog for some aversion therapy; and to contact the Guide Dogs for the Blind Association to see if there is any possibility of working with guide dogs.

My Experiences with Autism

Jerimie Goike

In this inspirational real-life account, author Jerimie Goike explains what life with autism has been like for him and his family. Diagnosed with autism when he was just eighteen months old, Goike describes his experiences with the disease from childhood to adulthood. He details how, with the help of his family, he beat the odds and created a successful and happy life for himself. He is now able to live on his own; he works as a telephone operator and is the owner of a disc jockey business.

I would like to begin by dedicating my story to my parents, who never gave up, and to the loving memory of my grandmother who became a very instrumental person in my life. I was diagnosed with autism at eighteen months by a military psychiatrist. My parents and I were living in Germany and my dad was serving in the

SOURCE: Jerimie Goike, "Autism from a Personal Perspective: A True Story of Beating the Odds and Winning," www.beachcenter.org, June 22, 2007. Reproduced by permission.

U.S. Army. After the diagnosis, the military made arrangements for us to return to the United States. We came back to Anniston [Alabama], which is my hometown, and we lived with my grandmother for a few months until we knew what to do and where to go. The Army told my parents that if they found a program that I could benefit from and it was located near a military installation, they would take care of the moving and relocation arrangements.

My first symptoms started with being nonverbal, rocking, sound sensitivity, and resistance to change. I also had some special abilities such as drawing, and I love music. I'm also visually impaired, which has bothered me since birth, but this has never had anything to do with my being autistic. I got my first pair of glasses after I turned a year old. After coming home from Germany, my mother started taking me to see some doctors, which seemed to do little good. Some would say, "Well, he's just a baby going through some phases and he will come out of it soon." Well, that wasn't enough for my mother. She knew there was something else wrong and nobody was listening yet. I still wasn't talking yet and I kept to myself a lot.

My grandmother took this pretty hard because the last time she saw me I was only a few months old. Now I was already walking and playing. I have a favorite story I like to tell. This story is about how my grandmother got me to talk. Every night when she put me to bed she would look at me and say, "Say mama, say mama" to me. She did this every night until one night I looked up at her and said, "Mama." That's how I finally began talking. This was the greatest joy I think my grandmother ever had and that's how my silence was broken. I was three years old and this was just the beginning. After having no luck with the doctors on trying to learn more about my situation my mother took me to the mental health center in Anniston and met with a social worker. After meeting with this person, my mother learned about the Autism Society of Alabama and she then learned about the TEACCH program at the University of North Carolina located in Chapel Hill. TEACCH stands for Treatment and Education of Autistic and related Communication Handicapped Children. We had tried a few programs while living in Anniston and had no success. These programs were only experimental at the time. I recall one scenario where they had me do a task and if I didn't cooperate or understand, I would get squirted with a water gun for punishment. There was another scenario where I was held down in a chair and I would be kicking and screaming because I didn't like the feeling of being restrained. None of these scenarios were working or providing any results and they all seemed to be set towards punishment rather than praise.

> **FAST FACT**
>
> Adults with autism say that finding a suitable job would improve their lives more than anything else.

My parents decided to move to North Carolina and enroll me into the TEACCH program. We moved to Fayetteville and my father was reassigned to Fort Bragg Military Reservation. They also put me into a preschool devoted to working with children with disabilities that also had ties to the TEACCH program. This program was very unique and in a class by itself. I really believe it was one of the only renowned programs in the whole country to provide a different approach to autism. I then went through three and a half years of various sessions with TEACCH to help improve my language, communication and social skills. The major emphasis was to train my parents on how to work with me and to have a better understanding of autism. They would give my parents a variety of tasks to perform with me at home because they felt the home was a better environment to learn in rather than sending me away to an institution. We would travel to the TEACCH center once a month for progress reports,

An Asperger's syndrome patient talks about his condition at the Judevine Center for Autism. Some adults with autism go on to live healthy, happy lives. (**AP Images.**)

meetings and to get new home assignments. The TEACCH center was a two hour drive from Fayetteville, and Chapel Hill is located outside of Raleigh.

There were also times where my therapist came out to our house to do behavioral observations, give ideas and suggestions. This was a very coordinated program between my parents, teachers, therapists and anyone involved with me. I would like to stress that TEACCH was not a cure for autism, but it can reduce the severity and make a lot of progress along the way. I believe what has helped me the most is the early diagnosis and going through early intervention programs. You really have to play your part and be supportive; both of these can be very valuable in a child's progress. What I remember most about the program is that everybody is in it together, and it's like a team.

After leaving TEACCH, it was recommended that I be placed in special education classes when I got ready to enroll in school, and that I would remain there until I graduated. I made a lot more progress than they expected. Although I was in special education classes most of my life, I did participate in regular education classes and after school programs. My high school was very helpful and supportive in making it possible for me to be a part of any program offered by my school that I desired to be involved in. I played basketball and became team manager. I took art and speech classes, which I enjoyed very much. After graduating from high school, I became involved with Vocational Rehab. I spent some time in Talladega at E.H. Gentry Technical Facility, which is affiliated with the Alabama Institute for the Blind and Deaf to study electronics. I then got a computer and taught myself how to use some of the Microsoft Office Programs. My efforts led me to getting a job and moving to Birmingham to live on my own and have an independent life.

I have lived successfully on my own for seven years. I worked for a non-profit organization called Special Education Action Committee (SEAC) as a clerical assistant and now I'm currently employed with the Alabama Department of Rehabilitation Services as a telephone operator. I've been with the agency for six years and it's been a very exciting time for me. I also own a Disc Jockey Business. I play at weddings, private parties, school dances and a variety of other entertainment functions. I've had a wonderful life and I wouldn't change a thing. If I could do it over again, I would. I would like to just say that learning from these experiences has prepared me for many challenges that came later in my life and it's kept me strong during these times. I would like to thank those who have helped and supported me through it all. If you've got yourself a dream, work hard and believe in yourself.

A Mother Finds Success for Her Autistic Child

Holly Robinson Peete, as told to Amy Elisa Keith

Amy Elisa Keith presents an interview with actress Holly Robinson Peete about her son's battle with autism. Peete noticed a significant loss of communication and connection with her two-year-old son after he received some vaccinations. She and her family tried a wide variety of treatment methods, and eventually her son RJ was able to take the battle into his own hands, improving socially and academically. Peete acknowledges her family's great success and hopes to inspire other families struggling with autism to seek the right treatment and continue to hope. Amy Elisa Keith writes about celebrities' lives for *People* magazine.

R J was born two minutes before his twin sister Ryan. He was the most delicious piece of butterscotch candy I had ever seen: chunky, laid-back, with these big eyes and dripping juicy lips. Something

SOURCE: Amy Elisa Keith, "Fighting Autism with My Son," *People*, vol. 67, June 4, 2007. Copyright © 2007 Time, Inc. Reproduced by permission.

drew me to him. When he started talking, "cow" was his first word. "Cow, cow," he would say, pointing his fat fingers at the picture. He and his sister were hitting all their developmental milestones right on time. He was sweet, had a great disposition and was always giving kisses and saying his few words. I will never forget that because one day he stopped. He went from saying "cow, cow" to nothing. Silence. Indifference.

RJ Is Different

That change happened when he was about 2 1/2, very soon after he had received his inoculations for measles, mumps and rubella. I noticed he ceased making eye contact and responding to his name without loud repetitive shouts. "RJ, RJ, RJ!" we would scream helplessly. I called Rodney, who was traveling. "Something's going on with RJ." And he said, "Maybe he can't hear. Get his ears checked." But that wasn't it. Rodney, like every man who felt helpless when he couldn't fix things, called again. "Everything's okay, right?"

But it wasn't. Together we took RJ to a specialist. She was a rigid, hard-looking woman who sat us in this icy office. The room was cold; the toys were cold. I hated everything about the place. Even the diagnosis was cold. She said, "Okay, here it is. He is a mid- to high-functioning autistic child. Here are a few phone numbers." With pessimism in her voice she said, "Unprompted, he will never say, 'I love you, Mommy,' or run to you and greet you at the front door." Something died in me the day RJ was diagnosed with autism.

Rodney and I cried for hours. What did we do wrong? I was in denial for a month. Then that became anger. I was ready to fight for RJ, but Rodney lagged behind. He and my mom were in denial. It was harder for him to fathom that something was wrong with his firstborn son and his namesake. I gave them an ultimatum: Get on board with RJ's treatment or go.

A Family Struggle

Autism can present an insurmountable strain on a marriage. And faced with the idea of divorce, I said to Rodney, "Quite frankly, I'm not trying to do this without you." At the time, we had a life strategist who counseled us and we still do, but during the worst part of the autism crisis, it was just the two of us battling it out.

We fought for RJ to stay in this world. Hours and hours of expensive, exhausting intervention: speech, occupational, vision therapies—all with endless waiting lists. There wasn't anything out there I wouldn't try: diets, acupuncture, hypnotism and enzyme treatments. Some yielded results; others were a waste of time and money. In all, we have probably spent about $500,000 in treatments.

When RJ was 3, I met the administrator of a preschool called Smart Start in Santa Monica where we enrolled RJ. It taught kids with mild mental retardation, Asperger's disorder, ADHD [Attention Deficit Hyperactivity Disorder]. She had them all. I sat in her office after hours of talking to people, going online, researching more treatments, and I just bawled. She was the first person who talked to me like I was going to get through this.

A Mother's Struggle

RJ's tantrums and behavior were hard to handle, especially when Rodney was away. He would self-stimulate with repeated movements, called "stimming" in autistic children, by flapping his arms. On a bad day he would literally fall down and cry inconsolably. I felt completely helpless. He only ate three things: pizza, French fries or pasta. The smell of anything else would throw him into a tantrum. People would say, "Can you control your child, please?" I would say, "My son is on the autistic spectrum." They didn't know what that meant. People asked, "Why don't you go to church anymore?" I made up excuses. I didn't go because I didn't want him to be disrup-

tive in church. I didn't want to see the looks on their faces. We worship in our own way.

Even friends did not understand. At playdates, RJ would come around and they would talk down to him. I lean on Jenny McCarthy and Tisha Campbell-Martin, who both have autistic sons. Jenny called me after her

RJ Peete (standing next to his father) has been triumphing over autism with the help of his family.

(AP Images.)

son was diagnosed. She said, "I'm sorry to call you, but . . ." and six hours later we were both laughing.

I used to wake up in cold sweats visualizing my child walking around homeless. My dreams were so scary, they pushed me into action. After trying countless therapies, we settled on something called Floor Time. We get on the ground and get up in RJ's face to force him to interact. We would both have toy cars, and I had to crash into his car. I refused to give him enough time to phase out.

The Work Pays Off

Never once did we think about sending him away. I chose a proactive, crazy-mama approach. Rodney had his own ways of teaching RJ. RJ went through a phase of repeatedly bouncing a basketball. So Rodney said, "If you're going to bounce the ball, then every five times you bounce it, you have to shoot it." We refused to let him bounce aimlessly. We are very goal-oriented. At 6 years old, our biggest goal for him was to have a conversation from start to finish. I say, "Hi," and RJ would say, "Hi, Mom. How are you?" I say, "I'm good and you?" and he would say, "I'm good too." Now RJ sets goals for himself.

> **FAST FACT**
>
> Gene studies focusing on African American families with an autistic member are uncommon.

I am just so proud of my boy. He is a happy 9-year-old about to enter the fourth grade at University Elementary School, a mainstream school. He struggles valiantly with subjects like math and reading and loves to write. Thankfully his classmates accept him just as he is. He blows us away with his ability to communicate now. The other day he said, "Mom, I know my name is Rodney Peete, but I don't want to play football. Is that okay? I want to play piano." I could barely get him to discuss his day with me two years ago.

Tantrums are now followed by RJ saying, "Okay, I'm going to play piano." He'll start playing beautiful arpeggios and scales. He will try any food now: salmon, brussels sprouts, salad. He leaves the athleticism to his younger brother Robinson, who competes with RJ for attention. His twin sister Ryan is never shy to step in for him. She mothers him, it's beautiful. And little Roman is just trying to roll with the big kids.

One Big, Happy Family

It's exhausting because we have to constantly love everyone, play up everyone's strengths and cheer for every little thing. But having a big family is important. I had Robinson five years after I had the twins because I didn't want Ryan to be the only one to have to take care of her brother. It was hard having to take care of my dad, who had Parkinson's, with my only brother. What if RJ can't live on his own?

RJ and I speak very frankly about autism. We treat it like a bully at school. I grapple with not wanting to make him a poster child, but he's a success story. I'm talking about it now because I want parents to have a glimmer of hope. Especially in the African American community, there's not a lot of information about autism. I want to take the scariness away.

Now that Rodney is retired, there are two of us to take care of the kids full-time. Even still, something as obvious as getting an eye exam for the kids got by me. Every day I'm packing backpacks, meeting teachers, scheduling treatments and heading up HollyRod, our nonprofit to improve the quality of life in Parkinson's patients.

And most amazingly, almost every single day for the last year, RJ, along with his three siblings, runs to meet me at the door with a kiss from those juicy lips saying, "Mom, you're home. . . . I love you." So much for never.

GLOSSARY

applied behavioral analysis (ABA) An autism treatment that uses behavior modification to increase appropriate behaviors and decrease inappropriate ones. Some behavior modification strategies include positive reinforcement and time-out.

Asperger's syndrome An autism spectrum disorder characterized by marked deficiencies in social skills and limited repetitive behaviors. Individuals with this syndrome often have normal to higher IQs.

atypical autism Another term used for pervasive developmental disorder—not otherwise specified (PDD-NOS).

autism spectrum disorders (ASD) A group of disorders or illnesses known as developmental disabilities. Autistic spectrum disorders include autistic disorder, pervasive developmental disorder—not otherwise specified (PDD-NOS), and Asperger's syndrome. These disabilities are distinguished by problems with social and communication skills of varying levels. ASDs typically start in young children and last a lifetime.

autistic disorder A developmental disorder characterized by impaired speech, impaired social and communication skills, repetitive behavior, and limited interests. Also known as classic autism or autism.

behavioral therapies Autism therapy that focuses on teaching a child specific skills and behaviors. This therapy employs a very structured learning environment using repetition and rewards.

biomedical treatments Medical treatments for autism that may include diet, vitamins, medications, and chelation, a process to remove heavy metals from the body.

Candida albicans Yeast that grows in the intestinal tract. This yeast can produce chemical compounds that can cause harm to the brain and the nervous system. Reducing the amount of this yeast in autism patients can lead to improvement of symptoms, including verbal and other communication skills.

casein Proteins found in human and cow's milk.

chelation A biomedical process used to remove heavy metals from the body, mainly lead, arsenic, and mercury. It has been theorized that autistic children have difficulty in naturally excreting heavy metals from the body. This process is one of the more controversial treatments for autism.

childhood disintegrative disorder A developmental disorder in which a child develops at a normal pace for two to four years, then loses communication and social skills. In many cases this disorder leads to severe disabilities. This condition is part of the PDD category of disorders.

clinical therapies Autism therapy provided by trained medical personnel, including physical therapy, speech therapy, and occupational therapy.

comorbid Two or more diagnoses that exist at the same time. Many autism patients have other conditions in addition to autism.

Crohn's disease A chronic disease that causes inflammation in the walls of the gastrointestinal tract. Individuals with autism often have accompanying problems with Crohn's disease and other inflammatory bowel conditions.

developmental therapies Autism therapy that focuses on individual interaction to help with the lack of basic developmental skills. Parents are often the main therapists with this approach.

dimethylglycine (DMG) A nutritional supplement that appears to help general well-being and, in some cases, communication skills.

discrete trial training (DTT) A form of applied behavior analysis therapy. A discrete trial is a specific teaching method that always has the same three distinct steps: beginning (antecedent), what the teacher does to make the student respond; middle (behavior), the response or lack of response on the part of the student to the beginning; and end (consequence), the teacher's response to the student's behavior.

DSM-IV *Diagnostic and Statistical Manual of Mental Disorders*, 4th ed. Covers all mental health disorders and contains diagnostic criteria, information, disorder characteristics, symptoms, and treatment options.

early infantile autism The name given to the category of symptoms discovered by Leo Kanner in 1938. Sometimes referred to as Kanner's syndrome.

echolalia When an individual repeats part or all of a previous word or phrase spoken by another person, usually without understanding what is said. This repetition is sometimes done immediately after hearing the word or phrase and sometimes much later: the next day, week, or month. This term is also referred to as echolalic speech.

encephalitis An inflammation of the brain caused by a viral infection. This brain condition has been associated with the development of autism.

fragile X syndrome A genetic condition resulting in mental retardation symptoms. It is caused by gene FMR1, located on the X chromosome. Autism can occur more frequently in individuals with this and other inherited medical conditions.

frontal lobe Front area of the brain; involved in the skills of planning, organization, problem solving, attention, personality, and other higher cognitive functions. Autism is believed to affect this area of the brain.

gluten Wheat, barley, and oat proteins.

methylation The metabolic process that makes a molecule larger by adding carbon. Studies have shown that autistic children have difficulty with this internal process.

MMR vaccine An immunization for measles, mumps, and rubella that is generally given near the age of one year. This vaccine has been the subject of much autism controversy regarding the mercury that is usually present in the chemical makeup of the vaccine. Mercury-free versions of the vaccine are now available.

nystatin	An anti-yeast drug used to kill yeast living in the intestinal tract. This drug is often used in conjunction with a gluten-free, casein-free diet for autism patients.
opioids	Chemical substances that have a painkilling action in the body, much like the action of morphine. These chemicals work by binding to opioid receptors in the gastrointestinal tract and the central nervous system.
organizational therapies	Autism therapy that focuses on the physical environment and daily routines. This therapy helps with an individual's ability to function on a day-to-day basis.
pervasive developmental disorder (PDD)	Disorders that affect the development of an individual's communication skills, social and personal interaction skills, and mental focusing abilities. This medical category includes autistic disorder, Asperger's syndrome, PDD-NOS, Rett syndrome, and childhood disintegrative disorder. PDD is often used as another term for autism, but PDD is not a diagnosis in and of itself. PDD is a class of conditions that includes autism. PDD-NOS, on the other hand, is a medical diagnosis.
pervasive development disorder —not otherwise specified (PDD-NOS)	Medical conditions that exhibit some, but not all, symptoms of autism. PDD-NOS is one of the autism spectrum disorders and can be referred to as atypical autism or atypical personality development.
phenylketonuria (PKU)	An enzyme deficiency that causes brain damage. This deficiency is present at birth and may be connected to the development of autism.
Rett syndrome	A genetic disorder that involves the loss of hand use, along with loss of communication and social skills. Repetitive hand movements and seizures are common. This condition, part of the PDD category of disorders, more often affects females.
savant	A person having both autism and savant syndrome. Also referred to as autistic savant.
savant syndrome	A condition of having both severe developmental disabilities and exceptional mental abilities; the outstanding mental

abilities usually occur in the areas of memory, mathematical calculations, art, or music.

speech apraxia　A speech condition caused by a lack of communication between the brain and the muscles that control speech. Children with a severe case of speech apraxia may be very hard to understand or may not be able to speak at all. This condition can accompany other autism symptoms, but can also occur in individuals without autism.

TEACCH　Treatment and Education of Autistic and related Communication-Handicapped Children, a therapy program started by the University of North Carolina that addresses needs in the areas of communication, social skills, and organizational skills.

temporal lobes　Two areas of the brain, one on each side at ear level. These lobes help distinguish different smells and sounds and are also responsible for short-term memory. The right lobe is for visual memory (pictures, faces) and the left lobe is for verbal memory (words, names).

thimerosal　An organic compound containing the heavy metal mercury that has often been used as a preservative in vaccines. This compound has been the subject of autism controversy because of the presence of mercury, which some believe is a factor in the development of autism.

tuberous sclerosis　A genetic disease that causes benign tumors to grow in the brain and on vital organs. Autism can occur more frequently in individuals with this and other inherited medical conditions.

vitamin B-6　When taken with magnesium, this vitamin has been shown to increase awareness, attention, and well-being in an average of 45 percent of autistic children.

Wing's Triad/ Wing's Square　The triad is a triangle of autism symptoms developed in the 1980s by Lorna Wing to help with the diagnosis of autism. An additional autism factor was added in the 1990s and Wing's Triad became known as Wing's Square.

CHRONOLOGY

1889 Psychologist M.W. Barr describes a twenty-two-year-old retarded male with a remarkable memory and mimicking speech patterns in a report titled "A Note on Echolalia, with the Report of an Extraordinary Case."

Early 1900s Psychologist Carl Gustav Jung introduces the basic personality types of extroverts and introverts. Using these categories, most autistic persons are subsequently classified as schizophrenic introverts.

1908 Psychiatrist Eugen Bleuler coins the term "schizophrenia."

1911 Bleuler coins the term "autism," from the Greek word autos, meaning "self." He invented the term to describe schizophrenic patients that closed themselves off and were very self-absorbed. He defines autism as an "escape from reality."

1938 Psychiatrist Leo Kanner observes the behavior of eleven children described as emotionally or intellectually impaired; among some of the children he finds behavior and abilities that do not reflect impairment.

1940s Bruno Bettelheim writes *The Empty Fortress*, a book about therapy sessions with autistic children. In the narrative he states that the children's disorder is due to their mothers being cold and aloof. He coins the term "refrigerator mothers."

1943 Kanner identifies autism as a medical condition in his scientific paper, "Autistic Disturbance of Affective Contact," describing it as a developmental disability that affects emotional and social understanding and skills. He also describes coexisting psychiatric conditions, including anxiety disorders, in his autism patients. Kanner reports an autism rate of 1 in 10,000.

1944 Independent of Kanner, Hans Asperger writes about a group of children he labels "autistic psychopaths." These children resemble the ones described by Kanner, except that their speech patterns were more like little adults. Asperger's work is published in German.

1950s Many people confuse the work of Kanner and Bettelheim, and the public believes that autistic children are the result of nonloving mothers.

Psychology professor Ole Ivar Lovaas begins working with older autistic children with limited success. He later switches to children under the age of five and stresses the implementation of treatment in the child's own home, with much greater success.

1964 Bernard Rimland publishes *Infantile Autism: The Syndrome and Its Implications for a Neural Theory of Behavior*. Rimland strongly disagrees with Bettelheim's parenting theory and stresses the idea of a biological basis for autism. Science begins viewing autism as a cognitive disorder.

1970 One in every twenty-five hundred American children is estimated to have autism.

1970s   In Sweden, the first autistic classes within special education are started.

1976   New types of disability categories begin to be introduced, such as specific learning disabilities, serious emotional disturbance, and others.

1980s   Autism research accelerates, debunking the theory of Bettelheim and finding basic physiological reasons for autism.

British psychiatrist Lorna Wing, at the Children's Neuro-Psychiatric Clinic in Göteborg, Sweden, establishes Wing's Triad, describing the major traits of autism.

1981   Wing first uses the term "Asperger's syndrome."

1987   Pervasive Developmental Disorder—Not Otherwise Specified (PDD-NOS) is added to the *Diagnostic and Statistical Manual of Mental Disorders*, revising the criteria for identifying autism and allowing more people to be included in the autism category.

1989   Asperger's work is translated into English.

1990   An estimated 4.7 out of every 10,000 American children are diagnosed with autism.

1991   Autism is added as a category for tracking American school children receiving special-education services.

1994   Asperger's syndrome is added to the *Diagnostic and Statistical Manual of Mental Disorders*.

1995   Over twenty-two thousand American school children receive special-education services for autism.

1998   In the United Kingdom, Dr. Andrew Wakefield publishes a paper reporting on twelve children who were diagnosed with autism and bowel disease after receiving the measles, mumps, and rubella (MMR) vaccine.

2002   Autism is estimated to increase at a rate of 10 to 17 percent each year.

2003–2004   Much-debated studies show that 60 out of every 10,000 American children are diagnosed with autism, which equals a ratio of 1 in every 166 children.

2004   Over 140,000 American school children receive special-education services for autism.

Ten coauthors of Wakefield's 1998 paper formally retract their support of his findings.

2005   An autistic boy dies after receiving controversial chelation therapy. His death is originally ruled accidental but is later found to have been caused by the wrong chelation agent.

2005   A study done in Japan shows continuing increases in the number of autism cases after an MMR vaccine is replaced with three individual vaccines. This study is taken by some as proof that the vaccine does not cause autism.

ORGANIZATIONS TO CONTACT

The editors have compiled the following list of organizations concerned with the issues debated in this book. The descriptions are derived from materials provided by the organizations. All have publications or information available for interested readers. Most of these publications are available online and can be downloaded for free in HTML or PDF format. The list was compiled on the date of publication of the present volume; the information provided here may change. Be aware that many organizations take several weeks or longer to respond to inquiries, so allow as much time as possible.

Autism Network International (ANI)
PO Box 35448
Syracuse, NY 13235-5448
http://ani.autistics.org

ANI is a self-help and advocacy organization run by individuals with autism. It advocates for civil rights and self-determination for all autistic people. ANI produces the newsletter *Our Voices*, published quarterly.

Autism Research Institute
4182 Adams Ave.
San Diego, CA 92116
(619) 281-7165
fax: (619) 563-6840
www.autism.com

This national organization focuses on research and information concerning autism and related disorders. The organization started Defeat Autism Now! (DAN!), an autism think-tank and conference group, and publishes the quarterly *Autism Research Review International Newsletter*.

Autism Society of America
7910 Woodmont Ave.,
Suite 300
Bethesda, MD
20814-3067
(301) 657-0881
toll-free: (800)
3-AUTISM
fax: (301) 657-0869
info@autism-
society.org
www.autism-
society.org

This organization is one of the largest autism support groups in the United States, with nearly two hundred chapters. It provides information and referrals to autism services nationwide. Its mission is to increase public awareness of autism and to help individuals with autism and their families deal with day-to-day issues. Its Web site offers a free e-newsletter, *ASA-Net*.

Autism Speaks
Two Park Ave.,
11th Floor
New York, NY 10016
(212) 252-8584
fax: (212)252-8676
contactus@autism
speaks.org
www.autism
speaks.org

This national organization promotes public awareness of autism and works to fund research into causes, prevention, and treatment of autism. Its Web site offers the *e-Speaks* newsletter, as well as news archives.

Cure Autism Now (CAN) Foundation
5455 Wilshire Blvd.,
Suite 715
Los Angeles, CA
90036-4234
(323) 549-0500
toll-free:
(888) 828-8476
fax: (323) 549-0547
www.cureautism
now.org

The main mission of this organization is the funding of research projects, education, and autism outreach. Its Web site provides the biannual newsletter *Advance*, as well as the *AGRE Family Newsletter* and *Cure Autism Now Research Overview*.

Family Voices
2340 Alamo SE,
Suite 102
Albuquerque, NM
87106
(505) 872-4774
toll-free:
(888) 835-5669
fax: (505) 872-4780
kidshealth@family
voices.org
www.familyvoices.org

Family Voices is a national organization providing information and education about family-based health care for children with disabilities. It offers multiple publications, including the newsletters *Friday's Child* and *Bright Futures*, all of which can be found on the Web site.

The Doug Flutie Jr. Foundation for Autism
PO Box 767
Framingham, MA
01701
(508) 270-8855
toll-free:
(866) 3-AUTISM
fax: (508) 270-6868
www.dougflutiejr
foundation.org

Founded by retired football player Doug Flutie, this organization's goal is to aid disadvantaged families with assistance in caring for children who are autistic. In addition to funding education and research, the organization also disseminates information on programs and services for individuals with autism.

MAAP Services, Inc.
PO Box 524
Crown Point, IN
46308
(219) 662-1311
fax: (219) 662-0638
info@maap
services.org
www.maapservices.org

MAAP is a national nonprofit autism organization for individuals with high-functioning autism spectrum disorders. It provides information and advice to families affected by such disorders. MAAP produces multiple publications, including the quarterly newsletter. The newsletter *MAAP*, all of which can be found on the Web site.

Dan Marino Foundation
PO Box 267640
Weston, FL 33326
(954) 888-1771
fax: (954) 423-5355
info@danmarino
foundation.org
www.danmarino
foundation.org

Founded by NFL Hall of Fame quarterback Dan Marino, this autism foundation supports treatment programs, disease research, and outreach services to children with developmental disabilities and chronic illnesses. In September 2005 the foundation established the Marino Autism Research Institute (MARI), a "virtual institute" dedicated to developing and implementing research programs, including training, clinical studies, and genetics.

National Autism Association
1330 W. Schatz Lane
Nixa, MO 65714
toll-free:
(877) NAA-AUTISM
naa@national
autism.org
www.nationalautism
association.org

This organization focuses on autism research, advocacy, education, and support for those affected by autism. Its goal is to educate society that autism is not a lifelong incurable genetic disorder but one that is biomedically definable and treatable. NAA also works to raise public and professional awareness of environmental toxins as causative factors in neurological damage that often results in autism or a related diagnosis. The Web site provides research findings, as well as press releases.

National Institute of Child Health and Human Development (NICID)
9000 Rockville Pike,
Bldg. 31, Room 2A32,
MSC 2425
Bethesda, MD
20892-2425
(301) 496-5133
toll-free:
(800) 370-2943
fax: (301) 984-1473
NICIDClearinghouse
@mail.nih.gov
www.nicid.nih.gov

This government institute, part of the National Institutes of Health, supports and conducts research on all areas of human development from infancy to adulthood. Health information publications can be found on the Web site or by contacting the institute directly.

National Institute of Mental Health (NIMH)
6001 Executive Blvd.,
Room 8184,
MSC 9663
Bethesda, MD
20892-9663
(301) 443-4513
fax: (301) 443-4279
nimhinfo@nih.gov
www.nimh.nih.gov

This government institute, part of the National Institutes of Health, covers all aspects of mental illness and behavioral disorders. The institute conducts and supports research; analyzes and disseminates information on mental health causes, occurrence, and treatment; supports the training of scientists to conduct research; and gives out information to the public concerning mental health and behavioral disorders. Pamphlets, fact sheets, and booklets can be found on the Web site or by contacting the institute directly.

National Institute of Neurological Disorders and Stroke (NINDS)
PO Box 5801
Bethesda, MD 20824
(301) 496-5751
toll-free:
(800) 352-9424
www.ninds.nih.gov/
disorders/autism/
autism.htm

This government institute, part of the National Institutes of Health, covers the neurological aspects of autism. The institute publishes numerous fact sheets that can be obtained through its Web site or by contacting the institute directly.

Organization for Autism Research
2000 N. 14th St.,
Suite 480
Arlington, VA 22201
(703) 243-9710
www.research
autism.org

OAR is an organization that uses applied science to answer questions that parents, families, individuals with autism, teachers, and caregivers confront daily. OAR funds research on treatment, education, and statistics, and publishes the *OARacle* newsletter, which can be found on its Web site.

FOR FURTHER READING

Books

Ann Boushey, *Talking Teenagers: Information and Inspiration for Parents of Teenagers with Autism or Asperger's Syndrome.* London: Jessica Kingsley, 2007.

Stephen M. Edelson and Bernard Rimland, *Treating Autism: Parent Stories of Hope and Success.* San Diego: Autism Research Institute, 2003.

Jennifer Elder, *Different Like Me: My Book of Autism Heroes.* London: Jessica Kingsley, 2006.

Michael Fitzgerald, *The Genesis of Artistic Creativity: Asperger's Syndrome and the Arts.* London: Jessica Kingsley, 2005.

Sam Frender and Robin Schiffmiller, *Brotherly Feelings: Me, My Emotions, and My Brother with Asperger's Syndrome.* London: Jessica Kingsley, 2007.

Mohammad Ghaziuddin, *Mental Health Aspects of Autism and Asperger Syndrome.* London: Jessica Kingsley, 2005.

Temple Grandin and Catherine Johnson, *Animals in Translation: Using the Mysteries of Autism to Decode Animal Behavior.* Orlando, FL: Harcourt, 2005.

Roy Richard Grinker, *Unstrange Minds: Remapping the World of Autism.* New York: Basic Books, 2007.

Lynn Kern Koegel and Claire LaZebnik, *Overcoming Autism.* New York: Penguin, 2004.

Kamran Nazeer, *Send in the Idiots.* New York: Bloomsbury, 2006.

Ann Palmer, *Realizing the College Dream with Autism or Asperger Syndrome.* London: Jessica Kingsley, 2006.

Wendy L. Stone, *Does My Child Have Autism?* San Francisco: Jossey-Bass, 2006.

Daniel Tammet, *Born on a Blue Day: Inside the Extraordinary Mind of an Autistic Savant: A Memoir*. New York: Free Press, 2007.

Periodicals

Mark Alpert, "The Autism Diet: Can Avoiding Bread and Milk Ease the Disorder?" *Scientific American*, April 2007.

Patricia Morris Buckley, "Dr. Bernard Rimland Is Autism's Worst Enemy," *San Diego Jewish Journal*, October 2002.

Diana Mahoney, "Intervention Can Improve Attention in Autism," *Clinical Psychiatry News*, October 2006.

Cammie McGovern, "Boy Wonder," *Reader's Digest*, August 2006.

Madhusree Mukerjee, "Insights: A Transparent Enigma," *Scientific American*, June 2004.

Vilayanue S. Ramachandran and Lindsay M. Oberman, "Broken Mirrors: A Theory of Autism," *Scientific American*, November 2006.

Philip E. Ross, "When Engineers' Genes Collide," *IEEE Spectrum*, October 1, 2006.

Joshua Tompkins, "Cracking the Autism Puzzle," *Popular Science*, vol. 267, no. 2, August 1, 2005.

Darold A. Treffert and Gregory L. Wallace, "Islands of Genius," *Scientific American*, June 2002.

Claudia Wallis, "Blame It on Teletubbies," *Time*, vol. 168, no. 18, October 30, 2006.

———, "Inside the Autistic Mind," *Time*, vol. 167, no. 20, May 15, 2006.

———, "What Autism Epidemic?" *Time*, vol. 169, no. 4, January 22, 2007.

Internet Sources

Hana May Brown, "'Intrusion' and Interaction Therapy for Riders with Autism." www.narha.org.

CBS News, "One Boy's Best Friend," May 16, 2005. www.cbsnews.com.

Andy Coghlan, "Autism Rises Despite MMR Ban in Japan," March 3, 2005. www.newscientist.com.

Caroline Fischer, "An Overwhelming Question," 2007. www.autism.org.uk.

Josh Fischman, "Origins of Autism," March 4, 2005. www.usnews.com.

A. Chris Gajilan, "Living with Autism in a World Made for Others," 2007. www.cnn.com/2007/HEALTH/02/21/autism.amanda/index.html.

Morton Ann Gernsbacher, Michelle Dawson, and H. Hill Goldsmith, "Three Reasons Not to Believe in an Autism Epidemic," *Current Directions in Psychological Science*, vol. 14, no. 2, 2005. www.psychologicalscience.org.

Thomas H. Maugh II, "Autism Study Finds Father's Age a Factor, No Similar Effect Seen with Mother," *Los Angeles Times*, September 5, 2006. *Boston Globe*, www.boston.com.

Medical News Today, "Males with Autism Have Fewer Neurons in the Amygdala, UC Davis M.I.N.D. Institute Researchers Find," July 21, 2006. www.medicalnewstoday.com.

Kelly Patricia O'Meara, "Vaccines May Fuel Autism Epidemic," June 9, 2003. www.worldnetdaily.com.

Evelyn Pringle, "Vaccine Fraud: Thimerosal-ADD-Autism Connection," February 2007. www.conspiracyplanet.com.

Lea Winerman, "Effective Education for Autism," *Monitor on Psychology*, vol. 35, no. 11, December 2004. www.apa.org/monitor/dec04/autism.html.

INDEX